Philemon
Among the Letters
of Paul

Philemon
Among the Letters
of Paul

A New View of Its Place and Importance

Revised Edition

JOHN KNOX

ABINGDON PRESS

NEW YORK • NASHVILLE

PHILEMON AMONG THE LETTERS OF PAUL

Copyright © 1935, 1959 by Abingdon Press

Library of Congress Catalog Card Number: 59-7248

SET UP, PRINTED, AND BOUND BY THE
PARTHENON PRESS, AT NASHVILLE,
TENNESSEE, UNITED STATES OF AMERICA

To Lois

Preface

WHEN PAUL SENT THE SLAVE ONESIMUS BACK TO HIS OWNER,
he placed in his hands what is universally acknowledged
to be one of the most charming letters ever written. So
charming, indeed, does it appear that one is likely to miss
how serious the little letter really is. So delightfully does
it read that one may easily overlook how carefully and
skillfully it was written. And so completely satisfying is
the letter when regarded as a generous appeal for another
that one may not see that Paul is asking—and very earnestly asking—something for himself. But it is in this
crucial fact that the secret of this letter and of its preservation by the churches really lies. It is my hope that the
following pages may serve not only to demonstrate the fact
but also to show that once it is grasped in all of its implications the letter becomes as a whole and in every part
more significant, and a new light is thrown both upon the
circumstances of its writing and upon its history as one of
the primitive documents of the Christian church.

The present book, first published in 1935, seeks to show

that there is sound reason for the opinion that it was the
position of importance achieved eventually in the Christianity of Asia by the former slave Onesimus which accounts for the inclusion of Philemon in the primitive collection of the Pauline letters. The importance of that fact,
if it should be proved, will be obvious to any student of
early Christianity. For the establishment of that thesis,
Chapters I, II, IV, and V are vital. Chapter III deals with
one difficult but highly interesting aspect of the relation
of Philemon and Colossians, and is only partly germane.
It is, besides, less important in its implications and less
assured in its conclusions. The suggestion it offers, however, fits so well into the picture this book presents that
I cannot help regarding it with favor. Still, the main thesis
of the book does not in any degree depend on it.

I make no apology for not undertaking to prove a number of positions, presupposed in this study, for which I
believe the argument has elsewhere been adequately stated.
In particular, may I say that along with virtually all
modern New Testament students I accept Philemon and
Colossians as genuine Pauline letters, but with an increas-
ing and always considerable number of them regard Ephesians as by a later hand. The work of Professor Edgar J.
Goodspeed upon the original character and function of
this Ephesian epistle provided the initial suggestion for
this study of Philemon, and my dependence upon it will
be apparent.

Thus far I have been largely repeating what I wrote in
1935 as part of the original preface of this book. I cannot
say to what extent the conclusions to which that study led

have been accepted by New Testament scholars. Since I owe so much to Dr. Goodspeed, I was particularly pleased by his immediate acceptance of my suggestion in Chapter IV about the primitive order of the Pauline letter corpus and of my argument in Chapter V for the use of Philemon by Ignatius, and I am deeply gratified that in one of his most recent books[1] he seems fully to accept the conclusions of this study about the connection of Onesimus with the formation of the corpus buttressing them with valuable additional arguments of his own. Albert E. Barnett had earlier taken much the same position.[2] I have reason to believe that at least a few other American scholars have found the hypothesis of this book attractive and, in part at least, convincing. It is also taken with some seriousness by H. Greeven in the latest revision of Dibelius' commentary. Among British scholars I think particularly of P. N. Harrison, C. L. Mitton, and C. F. D. Moule.[3] Both Harrison and Mitton I interpret as largely accepting the general argument, with whatever qualifications at particular points; Moule is more cautious. "It is thus possible, though not demonstrable," he writes, "that we are given a glimpse of a spectacular sequel to St. Paul's letter many years later."

[1] *The Key to Ephesians* (Chicago: University of Chicago Press, 1956).

[2] *The New Testament: Its Making and Meaning* (Nashville: Abingdon Press, 1946), pp. 79-92, 184-85.

[3] P. N. Harrison, "Onesimus and Philemon," *Anglican Theological Review*, XXXII (1950), 286-94. C. L. Mitton, *The Epistle to the Ephesians* (Oxford: Clarendon Press, 1951) and *The Formation of the Pauline Corpus of Letters* (London: Epworth Press, 1955). C. F. D. Moule, *The Epistles to the Colossians and Philemon* (Cambridge: Cambridge University Press, 1957).

That the "sequel" is not "demonstrable," I would agree, of course. I am convinced, however, that it is true—quite as much convinced as I was twenty-four years ago. This book as a whole is devoted to stating the grounds for that conviction, and I must not enter upon any defense of it now. But I cannot refrain from saying that in my judgment some of the critics of my conclusions have not given sufficient weight to the cumulative effect of the argument. An hypothesis, which has the virtues both of inner consistency and of relevance to a wide range of perplexing data, otherwise unrelated, and which, at every point out of many where it *can* be tested, is found to be at least possible—and often much more than that—such an hypothesis, even though it must in the nature of the case remain an hypothesis only, can make large claims to truth.

No major changes have been made in the new edition. Sentence structure has occasionally been altered in the interest of better style, and such errors in detail as had been called to my attention have been corrected. (No doubt some such errors still remain.) I have also amplified my earlier arguments at a few points, sometimes utilizing materials from my *Marcion and the New Testament* and from an article, "Philemon and the Authenticity of Colossians," first published in the *Journal of Religion*.[4] Many notes have been rewritten and others have been freshly composed in an effort to cover discussion of some of the

[4] Both of these publications, to be identified more exactly later, were by the University of Chicago Press. I am grateful to the editor of this Press for permission to use them, as well as for his generous cooperation in making this revised edition possible.

themes of this book since 1935. Quotations of the English New Testament are regularly from the Revised Standard Version. Where other published versions are used, they are designated. My own occasional translations or paraphrases will be, I think, sufficiently apparent as such.

The original printing of this work was very small. It is my hope that this larger edition will help make the little letter to Philemon, too much neglected or taken for granted, more interesting and significant to a larger circle of readers than those who saw the first publication.

JOHN KNOX

Contents

CHAPTER I

———•✦•———

The Letter to Philemon

I

THE FIRST SCENE IN THE DRAMATIC STORY OF THE LITTLE document known as "the Letter to Philemon" takes place in an unnamed city of the Roman Empire at a time somewhere near the middle of the first century of our era. Paul, the foremost Christian missionary, is in prison. As the story begins, he is saying good-by to a slave, Onesimus, who has evidently become a Christian under his influence and whom he is now dispatching to his owner, who resides apparently some distance away. It is clear that Paul has become very warmly attached to Onesimus and is reluctant to part with him. Finally, however, giving him a letter to be delivered to his master, he starts him on his journey.

To the composing of this letter Paul had devoted no little care, although he had not the slightest thought that it would survive the emergency which called it forth. But by a strange fortune it has come down to us, one of the most charming letters ever written. As translated in the Revised Standard Version of the Bible, the letter the slave carried read as follows:

15

Paul, a prisoner for Christ Jesus, and Timothy our brother,

To Philemon our beloved fellow worker and Apphia our sister and Archippus our fellow soldier, and the church in your house:

Grace to you and peace from God our Father and the Lord Jesus Christ.

I thank my God always when I remember you in my prayers, because I hear of your love and of the faith which you have toward the Lord Jesus and all the saints, and I pray that the sharing of your faith may promote the knowledge of all the good that is ours in Christ. For I have derived much joy and comfort from your love, my brother, because the hearts of the saints have been refreshed through you.

Accordingly, though I am bold enough in Christ to command you to do what is required, yet for love's sake I prefer to appeal to you—I, Paul, an ambassador and now a prisoner also for Christ Jesus—I appeal to you for my child, Onesimus, whose father I have become in my imprisonment. (Formerly he was useless to you, but now he is indeed useful to you and to me.) I am sending him back to you, sending my very heart. I would have been glad to keep him with me, in order that he might serve me on your behalf during my imprisonment for the gospel; but I preferred to do nothing without your consent in order that your goodness might not be by compulsion but of your own free will.

Perhaps this is why he was parted from you for a while, that you might have him back forever, no longer as a slave but more than a slave, as a beloved brother, especially to me but how much more to you, both in the flesh and in the Lord. So if you consider me your partner, receive him as you would receive me. If he has wronged you at all, or owes you anything, charge that to my account. I, Paul, write this with my own

16

hand, I will repay it—to say nothing of your owing me even your own self. Yes, brother, I want some benefit from you in the Lord. Refresh my heart in Christ.

Confident of your obedience, I write to you, knowing that you will do even more than I say. At the same time, prepare a guest room for me, for I am hoping through your prayers to be granted to you.

Epaphras, my fellow prisoner in Christ Jesus, sends greetings to you, and so do Mark, Aristarchus, Demas, and Luke, my fellow workers.

The grace of the Lord Jesus Christ be with your spirit.

The scene we were watching a moment ago lies patent enough in the letter itself, but any number of questions to which the letter gives no answer occur to one who watches it. One wonders, for example, how Onesimus happened to be with Paul. Had he also been under arrest? Or had he, perhaps, been sent by his owner with some message or gift for Paul or for one of Paul's companions in prison? We are not told, but since the letter contains at least two hints that Onesimus is not in favor with his master—he is said to have been "useless" or "unprofitable" to him, and there is a strong indication that he has caused his master some loss—it is not unnatural that his presence with Paul should always have been explained by the hypothesis that he was a runaway slave, who had previously wronged, perhaps robbed, his owner, and had either sought Paul out in some foreign city or had accidentally met him there. This account of Onesimus' being with Paul may or may not be true. As a tentative theory, it will serve as well as any of the several others which might be constructed on the meager facts we have. Still, it should be realized that it rests upon no explicit statement of the letter itself.

It is, then, this slave, possibly a runaway, whom Paul is sending to his master—and with a letter. What will the letter contain? We are almost sure before we open it—it will be a plea on behalf of the slave. It will be an appeal that the owner will forgive Onesimus and restore him to his former place in his household. Why should it not be such a letter? A runaway slave in the Roman society of the period was usually summarily dealt with.[1] He might be punished with any penalty the owner chose to impose. Onesimus, then, will need an advocate. Paul is in prison and cannot accompany him, but he can do the next best thing—he can write a letter. All of this seems so reasonable and inevitable that once we decide that the note was written to the master of a runaway slave, we are likely to feel that we possess the only clue needed for its complete interpretation. But in doing so we are taking quite too much for granted. Even if Onesimus was a runaway slave (which is by no means certain), it does not follow at all that Paul's letter is only an appeal on his behalf. And to read the letter with that assumption may mean missing its message or some important part of it. It is my conviction that this presupposition has often resulted in serious distortion of the otherwise plain meaning of the note. I do not for a moment deny that Paul may have been anxious

[1] Valuable general works on slavery in the Roman Empire are R. H. Barrow, *Slavery in the Roman Empire* (London, 1928), and H. Wallon, *Histoire de l'esclavage dans antiquité* (Paris, 1879). A special study by Erwin R. Goodenough ("Paul and Onesimus," *Harvard Theological Review*, XXII, 181 ff.) is interesting in this connection.

about Onesimus' safety or that he may be asking the owner to receive him kindly; I do assert that this is far from being the main point of the letter.

We are very fortunate in having among the letters of Pliny a document of about the length of Philemon, the purpose of which is clearly the same as that commonly ascribed to that letter. It is addressed to Sabinianus.

Your freedman, whom you lately mentioned to me with displeasure, has been with me, and threw himself at my feet with as much submission as he could have fallen at yours. He earnestly requested me with many tears, and even with all the eloquence of silent sorrow, to intercede for him; in short, he convinced me by his whole behavior that he sincerely repents of his fault. I am persuaded that he is thoroughly reformed because he seems deeply sensible of his guilt. I know you are angry with him, and I know, too, it is not without reason; but clemency can never exert itself more laudably than when there is most cause for resentment. You once had an affection for this man, and, I hope, will have again; meanwhile, let me only prevail with you to forgive him. If he should incur your displeasure hereafter, you will have so much the stronger plea in excuse of your anger as you show yourself more merciful to him now. Concede something to his youth, to his tears, and to your own natural mildness of temper: do not make him uneasy any longer, and I will add too, do not make yourself so; for a man of your kindness of heart cannot be angry without feeling great uneasiness. I am afraid, were I to join my entreaties with his, I should seem rather to compel than request you to forgive him. Yet I will not scruple even to write mine with his; and in so much the stronger terms as I have sharply and severely reproved him, positively threatening never to interpose again in his behalf. But though it is proper to say this to him in order to make him more fearful of offending, I do not say so to you. I may, perhaps, again have occasion to entreat you upon his behalf, and again obtain his forgiveness; supposing, I mean, his fault should be such as may become me to intercede for and you to pardon. Farewell.[2]

Now if the reading of this letter is followed by a fresh perusal of Philemon, a note of almost equal elegance and, we are convinced, of even greater skill, one will be struck with this difference: Given a common purpose, Pliny is more forthright, direct, and explicit than Paul. Pliny says exactly what we should expect such a note to say. Paul, on the other hand, does not say some things we should certainly expect and says others which seem scarcely relevant. Pliny cites the penitence of his protégé, devoting a full third of his letter to emphasizing it in various ways, while the rest of the note is made up entirely of repeated pleas for the master's indulgence and of arguments for clemency. But Paul says not one word about any repentance on the part of the slave and there is no explicit appeal for forgiveness or pity on the part of the master. In other words, the terms we should expect such a letter to contain in abundance are simply not there at all. This fact alone should lead us to suspect a rather deeper purpose in the letter than the obvious one generally assigned. Let us examine the letter with that possibility in mind.[3]

[2] Pliny *Epistolae* trans. Bosanquet (London, 1914), ix. 21.

[3] The Greek text of the New Testament adopted for this study is Westcott and Hort, *The New Testament in the Original Greek* (New York: The Macmillan Company, 1925).

II

Paul begins with the usual paragraph of address and greetings:

Paul, a prisoner for Christ Jesus, and Timothy our brother, to Philemon our beloved fellow worker and Apphia our sister and Archippus our fellow soldier, and the church in your house: Grace to you and peace from God our Father and the Lord Jesus Christ.

This paragraph we shall subsequently have occasion to look at in some detail. Now it is necessary only to point out that its quite formal character would have suggested at once to the first readers of Philemon that Paul was writing as an authoritative supervisor of churches to a church and to one of its members, and not as one mere individual to another.

This impression of formality is confirmed by the next section of the epistle (vss. 4-7), the so-called "thanksgiving." Paul Schubert in his definitive and illuminating study of the thanksgivings in the Pauline letters [4] has shown not only that they are invariably worked out most carefully and skillfully along the lines of a characteristic pattern, but also that in each case the thanksgiving sustains a very specific connection with what Paul plans to say in the body of the letter. Brief as Philemon is, it is remarkably normal in both of these respects. The usual formal pattern of the thanksgiving is followed, and the paragraph is clearly

[4] *The Form and Function of the Pauline Thanksgivings* (Berlin: Töpelmann, 1939). See also E. Lohmeyer, *Die Briefe an die Kolosser und an Philemon* (Göttingen: Vanderhoech and Rupprecht, 1930), pp. 173-74.

designed to prepare the way for the specific matter with which the rest of the letter is to be largely concerned. It is the overture in which each of the themes, to be later heard in a different, perhaps more specific, context, is given an anticipatory hearing. Note προσευχῶν (prayers), cf. vs. 22; ἀγάπην (love), cf. vs. 9; κοινωνία (sharing or partnership), cf. vs. 17: ἀγαθοῦ (good or goodness), cf. vs. 14; σπλάγχνα (heart or hearts), cf. vss. 12 and 20; ἀναπέπαυται (have been refreshed), cf. vs. 20; ἀδελφέ (brother), cf. vs. 20. In this opening section of his letter Paul celebrates the generous character of the slaveowner's relations with his fellow Christians. He has admitted them to a genuine "partnership"; he has "refreshed" their hearts. Paul himself has been encouraged by this "love," because (as soon appears) he too has something to ask. He thus leads up to a request which with consummate skill he now proceeds to state.

He begins by saying that although he feels that he has every right to demand what is due (ἐπιτάσσειν σοι τὸ ἀνῆκον), yet because of all that he knows of the slaveowner's generosity, he prefers rather to appeal to him— he appeals to him for his child (παρακαλῶ σε περὶ τοῦ ἐμοῦ τέκνου). The important question for the interpreter here is the force of the preposition "for" (περί). Is Paul appealing *on behalf of* Onesimus? Or is he simply asking *for* Onesimus? Study of the relatively infrequent cases in which παρακαλῶ was followed by this preposition in late Greek will show that περί often, if not usually, designated the content of the request. For example we are told by Appianus that the poor of Rome on one occasion asked

Caesar for land (τῶν ἀπόρων αὐτὸν ἐς Ῥώμην ἐπανελθόντα περὶ γῆς παρακαλούντων).[5] Other instances of this usage are to be found in the papyri; as, for example, Oxyrhynchus 1070, in which an Alexandrian husband writes to his wife: "The prayer which I previously made to all the gods for the preservation of yourself (εὐχὴ ἡ περί τε τῆς σωτηρίας σου) and our child and your brother and father and mother and all our friends now goes up to them with far greater force in the great Serapeum, and I beseech (παρακαλῶ) the great god Serapis for (περί) your life and that of all our friends and for the good hopes that are held by all mankind."[6] Paul himself uses the preposition (it happens in this case to be ὑπέρ) after παρακαλῶ only once in addition to the instance we are discussing. This is in II Cor. 12:8 (ὑπὲρ τούτου τρὶς τὸν κύριον παρεκάλεσα ἵνα ἀποστῇ ἀπ᾽ ἐμοῦ),[7] where the preposition, in view of the closely following ἵνα-clause, may well mean "for," or may be equivalent to "about" in some more general sense, but where "on behalf of" is clearly out of the question. It is demonstrably true that παρακαλῶ περί might mean "to ask for,"[8] and possible indeed that this was its

[5] Appianus, *Punic Wars,* 136.

[6] Arthur S. Hunt, *The Oxyrhynchus Papri* (London, 1910), VII, 227-29.

[7] G. A. Deissmann cites an interesting parallel to this passage in *Light from the Ancient East* (London, 1927), pp. 307-8. I Thess. 3:2, where the word means "to encourage," is not relevant.

[8] C. F. D. Moule (*op. cit.,* p. 21) writes that I take "the παρακαλῶ σε περί . . . of vs. 10 to mean 'I request you for . . . ,' as though Paul were not making a request *concerning* Onesimus but rather *for the gift of him.*" Professor Moule neither accepts nor rejects this proposal, but his sentence does not seem to me to state the relation between the two possibilities quite correctly. One does not need to decide that Paul is not making a

most frequent meaning. I submit that the whole context in Philemon all but demands that interpretation here; surely no one will argue that the alternative meaning of "on behalf of" is demanded, or even clearly indicated. Paul, with all possible delicacy, is asserting a claim upon Onesimus.

This claim he bases upon the fact that Onesimus is his child. He has given birth to him as "Onesimus" (τοῦ ἐμοῦ τέκνου, ὃν ἐγέννησα . . . Ὀνήσιμον).[9] Most of the commentators notice the case of Ὀνήσιμον and account for it by the attractive force of the relative ὅν. They thus translate it as though it were a genitive and in apposition with τέκνου. But to do so is to miss the whole point of the clause, which involves a play upon the word ὀνήσιμος (useful). Ὀνήσιμον as well as ὅν is the object of ἐγέννησα. "As Onesimus," Paul is saying, "he is my own child, for before his rebirth he was useless to you, but now he is useful to us both." Unless Ὀνήσιμον has this meaning, there is no point in the explanation of the pun in vs. 11. As to whether Paul gave the slave the name, as well as the character that made him worthy of it, we cannot be sure. In either case, Onesimus is now "himself" (αὐτόν). The pronoun αὐτόν is troublesome only so long as it is thought of as

request *concerning* Onesimus in order to recognize that he is asking *for* him. It may be argued, and agreed, that περί with the genitive always means "about," or "with reference to"; what I am saying is that after παρακαλῶ the "about" can often be sharpened. A request *for* Onesimus would certainly also be a request *concerning* him.

[9] This use of the terms "child" and "birth" is familiar in the mystery cults of the period. For examples see H. R. Willoughby, *Pagan Regeneration* (Chicago: University of Chicago Press, 1929). See also I Cor. 4:14-17.

merely personal, rather than intensive. "It is this new Onesimus—Onesimus really himself—whose case I am referring to you (ἀνέπεμψα), and now that I send him, I seem to be sending my heart."

The word ἀνέπεμψα is usually rendered "I send back." It is true that the word occasionally had that meaning, but apparently only very occasionally indeed. Its primary significance is obviously "send up," and in the New Testament period it was commonly employed to indicate the reference of a case from a lower to a higher court. It is used four other times in the New Testament and always with this meaning, three times in the Luke-Acts account of Jesus' trial and once in the same work's narrative of Paul's appeal to Rome.[10] That the term has the same legal connotation in the Philemon passage there is not the slightest reason to doubt. Paul is referring Onesimus' case to his legal owner for decision.

He has already more than hinted what the issue is upon which the owner must give his opinion (γνώμη). He now proceeds to state it more clearly. He wanted to keep Onesimus with him to serve in his master's place and was even thinking of doing so (ἐβουλόμην), when he decided that this would have made it appear that the owner had been forced to relinquish the slave, whereas Paul prefers that his acquiescence, here tacitly assumed, shall be voluntary. For perhaps, he goes on to say, that was why the slave was taken away for a short time that his master might come to sustain a permanent relation with him of an alto-

[10] Luke 23:7, 11, 15; Acts 25:21.

gether different kind—Onesimus should no longer be his slave, but his brother, dearest indeed to Paul, but dearer than before also to him, since Onesimus will be loved not only for himself (ἐν σαρκί) but "in the Lord."

The sentence which we have just paraphrased deserves somewhat longer inspection. It reads as follows: τάχα γὰρ διὰ τοῦτο ἐχωρίσθη πρὸς ὥραν, ἵνα αἰώνιον αὐτὸν ἀπέχῃς, οὐκέτι ὡς δοῦλον ἀλλὰ ὑπὲρ δοῦλον, ἀδελφὸν ἀγαπητόν, μάλιστα ἐμοί, πόσῳ δὲ μᾶλλον σοὶ καὶ ἐν σαρκὶ καὶ ἐν κυρίῳ. Both γάρ and διὰ τοῦτο [11] warn us that this sentence bears a close relation with the preceding one and can be understood only in the light of it. Paul has just indicated that he wanted to keep Onesimus but decided not to do so without the owner's consent (χωρὶς . . . τῆς σῆς γνώμης) in order that the latter's gift might be in every sense voluntary. "For," he proceeds, "perhaps it was on *that* account that he was taken away (ἐχωρίσθη; i.e., χωρὶς τῆς σῆς γνώμης[?]) for a little while." On what account? we ask. The natural answer would be, "In order that you might freely relinquish your claim to him forever." Everything in the context would lead us to expect some such conclusion; what we have is the interesting and highly ambiguous phrase αἰώνιον αὐτὸν ἀπέχῃς. This phrase is commonly rendered "that you might receive him back forever," and the sense of the clause is thus made to appear almost the

---

[11] Διὰ τοῦτο occurs in Paul's nine letters sixteen other times. In only a few of these cases is it even possible to think of the phrase as referring forward, and in each of those it much more probably looks back to the preceding sentence. Εἰς τοῦτο was Paul's way of indicating connection with a following final clause.

exact opposite of all that the preceding sentence, the γάρ, the διὰ τοῦτο, and the ἐχωρίσθη have led us to expect. It is important to notice, however, that even if ἀπέχῃς means "that you may have him back," in the ordinary sense, Paul hastens to qualify its force by adding "no longer as a slave." (There does not need to be a comma after ἀπέχῃς.) But it is highly doubtful that the term here had this simple sense. For one thing, it is a rare word in Paul, occurring only once besides (in Phil. 4:18, where again it has a special significance), and the ideas of "receive," "possess," and associated notions are invariably expressed by other words—not once by ἀπέχειν. We can suspect that Paul did not employ this word in Philemon, a letter manifestly so carefully composed, without conscious design. Needless to say, the term meant primarily "to hold, or keep, away," and in the first edition of this book I ventured to suggest the possibility that some trace of this meaning might be present here, Paul having used the antonym κατέχειν in the preceding sentence. In this suggestion I was probably mistaken. Ἀπέχειν, in its active form and transitive use, apparently must mean "to have or receive in full." Even so, the uniqueness of this appearance of the term in Paul suggests that he has a special meaning in mind, and this conclusion is confirmed by the use of the adverb αἰώνιον (forever), a term surely employed here in a religious sense: the owner was separated from his slave for an hour in order that he might thenceforth possess him *not as a slave,* but in a quite new sense, *forever.* Onesimus has now become his brother in Christ.

As such, Paul says, he is "dear especially to me and

how much more to you both in the flesh and in the Lord" (ἀγάπητον, μάλιστα ἐμόι, πόσῳ μᾶλλον σοὶ καὶ ἐν σαρκὶ καὶ ἐν κυρίῳ) . Both Lohmeyer and Moule take the superlative μάλιστα as elative—that is, as meaning simply "exceedingly," so that the comparative μᾶλλον can be understood as heightening its force. Moule cites Lightfoot as preferring "to treat it as an enthusiastic illogicality: 'most of all to me—more than most of all to thee.' " But why may we not take the superlative as well as the comparative with all seriousness, especially in connection with ἐν σαρκὶ καὶ ἐν κυρίῳ? The slave is to be dearest (μάλιστα) to Paul, even though he is to be dearer (μᾶλλον) *than before* also to the owner, being known and loved now, not only as a man, but also in the Lord. This proposal seems to be worthy of consideration but nothing of importance depends on its truth. The μάλιστα may represent simply a courteous exaggeration.

Paul asks that his protégé be admitted to the same partnership of which he feels himself to be a member.[12] As a transfer of ownership would normally have required,[13] he underwrites any debt of the slave to his owner, although he reminds the latter that he really owes Paul himself as well as his slave.[14] He acknowledges that he is trying to

[12] Προσλαμβάνειν was used regularly with κοινωνόν to mean "to take on as a partner." See Liddell and Scott, *A Greek-English Lexicon* (Oxford, 1934) , under προσλαμβάνω. Moulton and Milligan quote a sentence from P. Amh. ii. 100 (A.D. 180-211) : προσλάβετο τὸν Κορνήλιον κοινωνὸν τῆς αὐτῆς λίμνης κατὰ τὸ ἕκτον μέρος ἐπὶ φόρῳ. . . . *The Vocabulary of the Greek New Testament* (London, 1929) .

[13] A slave who is being sold is described in a contract of sale (Oxyr. 1290) as "free from external claim."

[14] What else can be the force of προσοφείλεις?

"make something" (ὀναίμην) out of his reader, and there is after all no genuine play upon the word unless what he hopes to "make" is Onesimus. He appeals to his reader to "relieve his heart," and could his use here of the strong word σπλάγχνα fail to recall the earlier sentence in which he had written that in sending Onesimus he was sending his heart (σπλάγχνα)? He closes his letter by expressing his assurance that he can rely upon his reader's obedience to do more than he has said. It is clear that this is no merely generous appeal on behalf of a slave boy in whom Paul had come to feel an interest. Paul's own affections and purposes are in the balance; he wants Onesimus to be returned to him.

This fact, the importance of which for the understanding of Philemon and of its subsequent history has in our opinion not been adequately recognized, has nevertheless more than once been suspected. Theophylact, commenting upon Φιλήμονι τῷ ἀγαπητῷ συνεργῷ . . . wrote, "If dear, he will forgive; if a fellow-worker, he will not retain (καθέξει) the slave, but will send him back for the ministry of preaching (ὑπηρεσίαν τοῦ κηρύγματος)." [15] Zahn is able to say, "At the most Paul no more than hints his desire that Philemon will give Onesimus his freedom," [16] but Jülicher is bolder and comes much nearer the truth when he writes,

The apostle now sends him back to his master, as he was bound to do, but entreats the latter to forgive him and to

---

[15] Commentary on the Epistle to Philemon.
[16] *Introduction to the New Testament* (New York, 1917), I, 453.

look upon him no longer as a slave but as a brother. Since he allows it to be seen how gladly he would have kept Onesimus beside him . . . it seems that he expected the liberation of the slave as the one service to which, for the sake of the gospel, he laid claim.[17]

And Ernst Lohmeyer confirms this view of the primary intention of the letter in every essential when he writes:

Paul would have a benefit (Nutzen) from Philemon; from this it cannot follow that Onesimus was again to be admitted into his previous slavery, but—the strongly accented "I" shows this—that Paul himself is to be the beneficiary (Nutzniesser). And he will be such only if Onesimus is set free for the service of the gospel. The benefit will then be in the strict sense a benefit "in the Lord." [18]

That the first readers of the letter understood it in some such way is almost beyond question.

That Philemon has not always been so understood is due to the force of the returning-slave stereotype as well as to our failure to give full value to Paul's own statement that he wants more than he says (εἰδὼς ὅτι καὶ ὑπὲρ ἃ λέγω ποιήσεις). Such a statement should warn the interpreter that every term and turn of the letter must be most carefully examined and that its real meaning may ultimately be found not in what it says unequivocally and definitely, but in what it suggests with some hesitation and indirection.

---

[17] *An Introduction to the New Testament* (London, 1904) , p. 125.

[18] *Op. cit.*, p. 191 (my own translation) . Lohmeyer does not emphasize, as I would do and as I believe vs. 13 requires that we should, the personal element in Paul's request. Paul wants the slave *returned to him* for "the service of the gospel." See also *op. cit.*, p. 173.

From the standpoint of the writer of such a letter, a measure of ambiguity at every particular point will be desirable, provided the total effect is clear and strong. Paul is making a large and unusual request; he wants to make it forcefully but not bluntly. Only when Paul's purpose for Onesimus is understood somewhat in the way we have been considering is it possible for the modern person to realize something of the flavor and weight which many of the words and phrases of the letter had at once to its original readers, especially since they knew, otherwise than by letter, circumstances of which we must be unaware. That we have not misunderstood Paul's primary object in writing Philemon I am convinced the closest scrutiny of the language of his epistle in the light of contemporary usage will amply demonstrate. As a matter of fact, the constant recurrence in the brief letter of words which had a definitely established legal or commercial connotation is itself enough to suggest that Paul's request had at least a quasi-business character. However informally, or even playfully, he may be using these terms, they occur to him as being appropriate in a letter which concerns the legal ownership or manumission of a slave.

It needs only to be added that if Philemon had the meaning suggested, it would have been regarded much more naturally than on the ordinary view, by both writer and readers, as dealing with more than a private affair and therefore as being not improperly addressed to others besides the slave-owner himself. The letter dealt with the release of a slave for religious service and was worthy of being read to the church, to which the owner belonged. It is also important to observe that if Philemon was concerned with a man's entrance upon a career of this kind, a man who may subsequently, for all that we know to the contrary, have attained eminence, the letter stood from the start a better chance of preservation than if it dealt with the return of an otherwise unknown slave to his master.

III

So far I have assumed the authenticity of Philemon and have passed over the matter of the time and place of its writing. The genuineness of the letter is so well established as to require little discussion, and the other matter is so uncertain as to call for too much. Any attempt to identify time and place would involve consideration of the whole question of the movement and chronology of Paul's life—a question not answerable with certainty or precision on the basis of our available materials. The meagerness of Paul's own autobiographical references accounts for our inability to reconstruct on the ground of his letters a really satisfactory biography, and the record of his career in Luke-Acts is not always trustworthy and is certainly not adequate. But all of that is beyond the province of this essay. Besides, it is doubtful if knowledge of Paul's exact situation at the time would increase substantially our ability to understand Philemon. The essentials are in the letter itself: Paul is in prison "for the good news," but hopes soon to be released, when he will resume his work. Meantime, his "fellow-workers" are apparently busy, and the propagation of the movement is going forward. On the whole, it seems most likely that he was not very far from the place of residence of his readers, and if that place was Laodicea or Colossae, as seems certain for reasons to be subsequently cited, the name of Ephesus suggests itself; but no assurance is possible.[19]

Very few scholars have ever denied the authenticity of Philemon.[20] The little letter bears in itself every mark of genuineness. It is, however, the matter to which we now turn our attention—the close and intricate relationship that Philemon sustains with Colossians—which gives it, as well as Colossians, its most impressive validation. Philemon alone might conceivably have been invented—although with what possible motive one finds it hard to imagine—but Philemon considered with Colossians could not. Colossians and Philemon together are more than two letters: they are two letters related to each other in a manner quite too remarkable to have been deliberately devised. Together they bring us a living moment in the experience of a Christian community in an ancient Asian city, a moment which no conscious artistry could so convincingly have created.

[19] Except that I see no adequate ground for even questioning the literalness of Paul's references to his "bonds," I find myself agreeing with Goodenough, *op. cit.*, p. 183: "If the reference to bonds is to be taken literally, it would appear that the imprisonment was much more probably one of the frequent and less serious detentions which Paul mentions in II Corinthians 11:23. The Ephesian imprisonment proposed by Deissmann would fit into the picture very nicely (*Light from the Ancient East* [1927], pp. 237 ff.)." For a full discussion of this possibility see G. S. Duncan, *St. Paul's Ephesian Ministry* (New York: Charles Scribner's Sons, 1930).

[20] For brief statements of this negative case see F. C. Baur, *Paul the Apostle* (London, 1875), pp. 80-84, and W. C. van Manen, "The Epistle to Philemon," *Encyclopedia Biblica* (New York, 1902). H. J. Holtzmann regarded parts of the letter as subsequent interpolations ("Der Brief an den Philemon," *Zeitschrift für wissenschaftliche Theologie*, XVI, 428 ff.).

CHAPTER II

Philemon and Colossians

I

THAT A CLOSE CONNECTION OF SOME KIND EXISTED FROM
the beginning between the two letters of Paul, to the
Colossians and to Philemon, has always been recognized.
Even the most casual reader cannot miss the more obvious
signs of that connection. In each Paul represents himself
as being in prison. The slave Onesimus, whose return to
his master provides the occasion of Philemon is mentioned
in Colossians as the companion of Tychicus, the bearer of
that letter, and moreover is said to belong in some way
to the Colossian church community (ὅς ἐστιν ἐξ ὑμῶν) .[1]
The readers of Colossians are asked to transmit to a certain
Archippus a special injunction from Paul, but Archippus
is one of the recipients of Philemon. Again, the readers of
both letters are greeted through Paul by the same five
individuals, Epaphras, Aristarchus, Mark, Demas, and

[1] Col. 4:7-9.

34

Luke, and probably also by a sixth, Jesus Justus.[2] Such facts ase these point unmistakably to the conclusion that these two letters were written at approximately the same time, were dispatched by the same messengers, and directed to the same or neighboring communities. So far as we are aware, this conclusion has never been questioned except by those who deny, entirely or in large part, the authenticity of either or both of the epistles.

The connection of the two letters, however, is not merely one of external circumstance. It is one of purpose and meaning. The whole of Colossians is more or less overshadowed by Paul's concern about Onesimus. We shall notice only the more explicit indications of that concern as they appear toward the end of the letter, although one can hardly pass by the χειρόγραφον in Col. 2:14, a figure which may so well have been suggested by Paul's having just given his bond in Philem. 19 (ἐγὼ Παῦλος ἔγραψα τῇ ἐμῇ χειρί). After leading up to the statement in Col. 3:11 that the status of "free" or "slave" is of no great importance, but Christ is everything and in us all, Paul devotes a paragraph to emphasizing "tenderness of heart (σπλάγχνα), kindness, humility, gentleness, forbearance," giving the exhortation, "You must bear with one another and forgive one another, if anyone has reason to be offended with anyone else. Just as the Lord has forgiven

[2] That the name of Jesus Justus is omitted from the text of Philemon by scribal error is plausibly argued by Ernst Amling, "Eine Konjectur im Philemonbrief," *Zeitschrift für die Neuestestamentliche Wissenschaft*, X, 261.

you, so you must forgive." [3] In connection with this passage it may be noticed that the word σπλάγχνα, which occurs twice in Philippians and twice in II Corinthians (1-9), Paul's most affectionate letters, occurs nowhere else except at this point in Colossians and three times in Philemon.

In the following paragraph, Col. 3:18–4:1, Paul comes closer to the point. He cites the relations of husbands and wives and of fathers and children, disposing of them all in three or four half-hearted sentences, in order to make a statement about the relations of slaves and masters, twice as long and many times more vigorous. This appearance of the so-called *Haustafel* (a table of household duties) in Colossians, alone among Paul's letters, cannot be easily explained apart from Philemon.[4] This pattern, common among Stoic and later Christian writers, is employed because Paul does not wish to address himself too abruptly to the slaves, whom his other letter and its hoped for consequences might well demoralize. Besides, he was probably eager to assure the masters that although in Philemon he had expressed himself strongly on behalf of Onesimus, still he was by no means encouraging disloyalty among slaves.

[3] From the translation of E. J. Goodspeed, *The New Testament: An American Translation* (Chicago: University of Chicago Press, 1923), Col. 3:13.

[4] For a discussion of this pattern see Karl Weidinger, *Die Haustafeln* (Leipzig, 1928). It is interesting to read in Toussaint, *L'epitre de Saint Paul aux Colossiens* (Paris, 1921), p. 189: "What reason has led Paul to speak of domestic duties? Perhaps the desire to plead again for the forgiveness of Onesimus by Philemon" (my translation). See also Lohmeyer, *op. cit.*, p. 155, and Dibelius, *An Die Kolosser, Epheser, an Philemon* (Tübingen, 1937), p. 35.

But let us not press the point, and let us suppose that Paul included the *Haustafel* without reference to any concrete situation among the readers of Colossians. It was a conventional thing to do, appropriate on general grounds, and so for no other reason he did it (although this is just the reason, it might be urged, why Paul, being Paul, might have been expected *not* to do it); but even so, can we conceive of him as actually addressing himself, in however formal or conventional a manner, to the slaves and masters at Colossae and not having particularly in mind as he did so the case of Onesimus, the slave whom he is that very day sending to his master, a member of the very church to which the epistle is to be read? It seems utterly impossible. If Colossians is an authentic letter, Paul must have been thinking about Onesimus as he wrote about the slaves and masters at Colossae. He could not have avoided doing so if he had wished.

That this passage was written with special reference to this slave is strongly indicated, not only by the disproportionately long treatment of master-slave relations, but also, and more particularly, by Col. 3:25. What can this statement mean otherwise? Paul is urging obedience and industry upon slaves and concludes by saying to them, ὁ γὰρ ἀδικῶν κομίσεται ὃ ἠδίκησεν, καὶ οὐκ ἔστιν προσωπολημψία. This final sentence in Paul's address to the slaves at Colossae is rendered by Goodspeed: "For the man who wrongs anyone will be paid back for the wrong he has done; there will be no exceptions." Moffatt translates: "For the wrong-doer will be paid back for his wrongdoing—there will be no favour shown." [5] And *The Twentieth Century New Testament* reads: "Those who do wrong will reap the wrong they have done; there will be no partiality." [6] The Revised Standard Version seems in a way to combine all three of these: "For the wrongdoer will be paid back for the wrong he has done, and there is no partiality." The statement is perplexing because, although evidently addressed to the slaves, it would seem to belong more appropriately in an exhortation to masters. Slaves are not accustomed to expect favor and partiality. Surely it would appear more fitting to say to them, "The one who does good will receive his reward, and there will be no discrimination against you because you are slaves."

The abnormality is so apparent that commentators almost universally from the time of Chrysostom have been troubled by the passage and have been divided in their judgment as to whether it may not actually have been the masters rather than the slaves to whom reference is being made. "It is possible that in ἀδικῶν," says Dibelius, "the master of the slaves is to be seen." [7] T. K. Abbott, in the *International Critical Commentary,* takes this position without equivocation:

The first clause is, of course, a general maxim, but the application here chiefly intended appears from the words οὐκ ἔστιν προσωπολημψία, which presuppose that the person punished is one higher in position. . . . Hence ἀδικῶν in the

[5] *A New Translation of the New Testament* (New York: Harper and Bros., 1922) , Col. 3:25.

[6] New York: Fleming H. Revel, 1904.

[7] *Op. cit.,* p. 36.

present case is the master, and the words are designed to encourage the slave to regard himself as the servant of Christ, and as such not to be disheartened by unjust treatment, knowing that before the final tribunal there will be no respect of persons. So Theodoret, . . . But Chrysostom, Bengel and others suppose the ἀδικῶν to be the slave.[8]

As a matter of fact, it would not occur to any reader that the passage refers to anyone else but the slave, were it not for the difficulty of understanding how in any generalized code the word προσωπολημψία could be applied to him. But is the Colossian *Haustafel* such a code, a set of merely general admonitions? We have seen good reason for suspecting that it is not. And now one remembers the case of a particular Colossian slave who has in fact "wronged" (ἠδίκησεν) someone (Philem. 18), and it becomes clear that the ἀδικῶν of Col. 3:25 may well be an allusion to that same individual. Indeed if this is not true, a surprising coincidence is involved—Paul makes in one letter a rather strange reference to what will happen to any slave at Colossae who wrongs anyone, and in another letter, written at the same time, alludes to a particular slave in that same locality as having wronged his owner—and there is no connection between the two references! It is, then, Onesimus who must pay for the wrong he has done, and no exception will be made. Paul has assumed his obligations, but that does not mean that he will not have to make them good.

[8] *The Epistles to the Ephesians and to the Colossians* (New York: Charles Scribner's Sons, 1905) , p. 296.

Upon this particular point I do not want to insist, but of the general view that Col. 3:18–4:1 reflects the concrete facts of Onesimus' case, the Epistle to the Ephesians furnishes, I believe, quite remarkable confirmation. As I have already indicated, I take the position held by the majority of critical students, that this epistle was written, not by Paul himself, but by a great disciple of the apostle a generation perhaps after the latter's death. The many grounds for this view can be found stated in any "Introduction" to the New Testament, and I do not intend to argue the case.[9] But two of these grounds need to be mentioned in the present connection. The first is the general nature of the address of the document and the generalized character of its contents. It was not sent to a particular congregation or to a definite group of congregations, as were the other letters of Paul, but to the church at large or, at any rate, to the church in some general area; and to many students of the early church it seems unlikely that the occasion for such a letter had arisen as early as Paul's own time. The other ground is the dependence of the document upon Colossians. Ephesians is really a rewriting of the other letter; and many scholars find this fact more readily explicable if a later Paulinist,

[9] See, for example, James Moffatt, *Introduction to the Literature of the New Testament* (New York: Charles Scribner's Sons, 1923), pp. 373-94. See also Dibelius, *An die Klosser, Epheser, an Philemon* (Tübingen: Mohr, third edition, 1953), pp. 56-57, 83-85; C. R. Bowen, "Ephesians Among the Letters of Paul," *Anglican Theological Review,* October, 1953, pp. 279 ff.; and F. W. Beare in *The Interpreter's Bible,* X, 597-607. For an able summary of the arguments see C. L. Mitton, *The Epistle to the Ephesians* (Oxford: Clarendon Press, 1951), pp. 7-24. The traditional position is also often and ably defended.

rather than Paul himself, is the author. Now this dependence on Colossians, as well as the "general" character of Ephesians, are acknowledged even by those who defend its Pauline authorship. It is agreed by all that Ephesians, whoever wrote it, is under one very important aspect a generalized edition of Colossians. The author, then, will be expected to omit or alter anything in Colossians which reflects the particular concrete situation in the Colossian church.

We are especially interested in Col. 3:18–4:1; but it may be worth noting that in the Ephesians passage (2:15) corresponding to Col. 2:14 we find τὸν νόμον τῶν ἐντολῶν ("the law of the commandments") instead of the striking χειρόγραφον, and that in Eph. 4:2 (or elsewhere in Ephesians) the σπλάγχνα of Col. 3:12 does not appear. These may be merely accidental divergences, but the phenomena of Eph. 5:22–6:9 cannot be so explained. It is clear that this passage is based upon the paragraph in Colossians we are now examining. Here are the corresponding sections of the two letters:

Col. 3:18–4:1	Eph. 5:22–6:9
Wives, be subject to your husbands, as is fitting in the Lord. Husbands, love your wives, and do not be harsh with them.	Wives, be subject to your husbands, as to the Lord. For the husband is the head of the wife as Christ is the head of the church, his body, and is himself its Savior. As the church is subject to Christ, so let wives also be subject in everything to their husbands.

41

Husbands, love your wives, as Christ loved the church and gave himself up for her, that he might sanctify her, having cleansed her by the washing of water with the word, that the church might be presented before him in splendor, without spot or wrinkle or any such thing, that she might be holy and without blemish. Even so husbands should love their wives as their own bodies. He who loves his wife loves himself. For no man ever hates his own flesh, but nourishes and cherishes it, as Christ does the church, because we are members of his body. "For this reason a man shall leave his father and mother and be joined to his wife, and the two shall become one." This is a great mystery, and I take it to mean Christ and the church; however, let each one of you love his wife as himself, and let the wife see that she respects her husband.

| Children, obey your parents in everything, for this pleases | Children, obey your parents in the Lord, for this is right. |

the Lord. Fathers, do not provoke your children, lest they become discouraged.

"Honor your father and mother" (this is the first commandment with a promise), "that it may be well with you and that you may live long on the earth." Fathers, do not provoke your children to anger, but bring them up in the discipline and instruction of the Lord.

Slaves, obey in everything those who are your earthly masters, not with eyeservice, as menpleasers, but in singleness of heart, fearing the Lord. Whatever your task, work heartily, as serving the Lord and not men, knowing that from the Lord you will receive the inheritance as your reward; you are serving the Lord Christ. For the wrongdoer will be paid back for the wrong he has done, and there is no partiality (ὁ γὰρ ἀδικῶν κομίσεται ὃ ἠδίκησεν, κὰι οὐκ ἔστιν προσωπολημψία).

Slaves, be obedient to those who are your earthly masters, with fear and trembling, in singleness of heart, as to Christ; not in the way of eyeservice, as men-pleasers, but as servants of Christ, doing the will of God from the heart, rendering service with a good will as to the Lord and not to men, knowing that whatever good anyone does, he will receive the same again from the Lord, whether he is a slave or free (ἐάν τι ποιήσῃ ἀγαθόν, τοῦτο κομίσεται).

Masters, treat your slaves justly and fairly, knowing that you also have a Master in heaven.

Masters, do the same to them, and forbear threatening, knowing that he who is both their Master and yours

43

is in heaven, and that there
is no partiality with him
(προσωπολημψία οὐκ ἔστιν).

It is interesting to note that every major difference in
form between the two sections can be best accounted for by
the fact that in Colossians Paul is writing with reference to
a particular concrete situation—the case of Onesimus and
its indubitable social complications—whereas the author of
Ephesians obviously is not. We have seen that in Colossians
the discussion of master-slave relations is of altogether dis-
proportionate length and of manifestly keenest interest to
the writer. We have seen the ground for this; but no such
ground would exist for the writer of Ephesians. He very
naturally felt that the passage in Colossians was out of proportion and corrected the matter by amplifying many times
over the treatment in Colossians of the more intimate
family relations. But when he came to write about slaves,
he evidently felt that the corresponding section in Colossians was on the whole satisfactory. He therefore virtually
repeats it—except for one sentence, Col. 3:25. This he
altered at two points: for ἀδικῶν he writes ποιήσῃ ἀγαθόν
as the smoother reading with κομίσεται; and he transposes
προσωπολημψία to what apparently seemed to him to be its
appropriate place, in the exhortation addressed to the
masters. In other words, he altered the slave section in
Colossians at the two points where, if we are right, it
touched specifically the case of Onesimus. He altered it
because apart from the concrete situation to which it
originally referred, the verse is scarcely intelligible.

44

In Col. 4:9 Paul becomes even more explicit, recom mending Onesimus by name to the Colossians as a "dear, faithful brother," one of their own number. And that Paul's interest, expressed in almost the last sentence of the epistle, that they should read "the letter from Laodicea" and that Archippus should discharge his "service," had no connection with Onesimus, I find it impossible to conclude. On the contrary, it is only when one sees in these closing sentences of Colossians the climax of his appeal for Onesimus that they become intelligible at all. Let us look at these sentences more minutely.

II

In Col. 4:16 there is evidence that at about the same time as that letter, Paul wrote and sent another communication which he there describes as τὴν ἐκ Λαοδικίας. In my opinion there is a probability approaching certainty that this letter was our Philemon.[10] Otherwise, we have no explanation of what soon becomes a whole series of amazing coincidences. In Colossians we learn that Paul is writing another letter, which he discribes as "the letter from Laodicea," a city not more than a dozen miles from Colossae and the metropolis of the Lycus valley area, in which Colossae was located. We possess a letter—Philemon— which on other grounds entirely we had determined was written by Paul at the same time and sent to this same

[10] This view is stated by Karl G. Wieseler, *Chronologie des Apostolischen Zeitalters* (Göttingen, 1848), pp. 431 ff., and has recently been very persuasively argued by E. J. Goodspeed, *New Solutions of New Testament Problems* (Chicago, 1927) and *The Meaning of Ephesians* (Chicago, 1933), pp. 6 ff.

territory. Can we escape the conclusion that it is the same letter? If it is not, we must assume that Paul wrote a third letter at this same time and sent it also to this area. But that is intrinsically unlikely—why so many letters to the same people? Besides, there is no independent evidence whatever for the existence of this third letter. If it ever existed, it has been completely lost. But would it have been lost? Would not a letter so definitely designated by Paul himself surely have survived?

The full force of this difficulty has often not been felt because of the existence of Ephesians. But for those who regard Ephesians as post-Pauline—and that means the majority of critical students of the New Testament—there is no such recourse. Indeed, even for others this recourse is not easy. We are confronted inescapably with the question why Philemon should have been preserved, but a letter sent at the same time and called particularly to the attention of the readers of Colossians should have been allowed to drop from sight. Was such a letter not destined from the beginning to preservation as a companion letter of Colossians? But Philemon, as we shall see later,[11] was so preserved. It was no doubt partly due to its close connection with Colossians that this brief and apparently personal note survived. Again, the mention of Archippus in Col. 4:17 is such as to suggest some connection between him and "the letter from Laodicea": "You read the letter from Laodicea, and say to Archippus, 'See that you fulfill the διακονία you have received.' " But Archippus was one of the recipients of Philemon.

[11] See below, pp. 85 ff.

46

What makes the identification of this letter as Philemon even more certain, however, is the fact that it enables us to understand why Paul is so eager that the Colossian Christians should read this "letter from Laodicea" that he all but closes his epistle with that injunction. He has already in this Colossian letter appealed indirectly for Onesimus; he has thus prepared his readers for the direct appeal which his other letter, our Philemon, contained. But the Colossians must be informed of that letter and instructed to read it. It is only upon the assumption that the "letter from Laodicea" is our Philemon that the closing sentences of Colossians can be understood at all. Otherwise, Paul having led up to the final and logical point, stopped just short of it. As we approach the end of Colossians, we expect some reference to Philemon, Paul's other letter. We actually find reference to *a* letter, "the letter from Laodicea." The conclusion that the letter so described is Philemon seems all but inevitable. Let me put the matter just a little differently. There is only one instance in Paul's correspondence of two letters clearly written at the same time and sent to the same or neighboring communities. There is also only one instance of Paul's referring in one letter to another as being written and sent at the same time and to the same readers. This one letter is one of the two involved in the other instance. Is it not clear that the burden of proof must be carried by those who deny the obvious conclusion that the letter we hear about is the letter we actually have?

But how could our letter Philemon have been described as "from Laodicea"? The answer that suggests itself at once is that it was addressed to Laodiceans, that Philemon, Apphia, Archippus, Onesimus, and "the church that meets in your house," all belonged there. Unfortunately, however, this seems not to have been true. In fact, the case for the view that the final recipients of Philemon were Colossians is quite as strong as for the view that it is "the letter from Laodicea." Stated as briefly as possible, it is as follows:

1. Onesimus is alluded to in Col. 4:9 as ἐξ ὑμῶν and the reference to Archippus in 4:17 is on the whole most naturally interpreted as indicating his residence in Colossae. It may be urged that ὑμῶν (in 4:9) is used in a broad way to include Laodiceans also, since the letter is to be read there as well as in Colossae (4:16). That is, of course, possible, but hardly likely, since throughout the letter the plural second person pronoun is consistently used to designate the Colossians, in two cases the Laodiceans being sharply distinguished from them (2:1 and 4:13). Similarly, the Archippus of 4:17 may have been a Laodicean, but the more natural reading of the passage would, we are inclined to believe, suggest his residence in Colossae. After all, his connection is not with "Laodicea" but with the "letter from Laodicea," which is actually to be read in Colossae. It is only when we start by assuming that the "letter from Laodicea" must also have been a letter to Laodicea that we are forced to see connection with the letter as involving connection with the city. But to start with that assumption is to beg the very question we are now discussing. The claim that if Archippus had been a Colossian, Paul would have addressed himself directly to

him in Col. 4:17, rather than instructing the church to speak to him, is negatived by the fact that elsewhere in the letters individuals are spoken of in the third person who are clearly members of the church being addressed. I am of the opinion that the references both to Onesimus and to Archippus in Colossians, when looked at without presuppositions of any kind, would suggest Colossae as the place of residence almost certainly for Onesimus, more probably than not for Archippus.

2. The letter Philemon gives its readers no direction to forward it to Colossae. But if it was sent to Laodicea and was to be interchanged with Colossians, would we not expect some such direction—some hint, at least, that the church at Colossae was also intended to read the note, especially as the phrase τὴν ἐκ Λαοδικίας surely would have suggested to the Colossians that the letter referred to was going to reach them in its normal course? And if Philemon was sent to the church at Laodicea, would we not have expected it to give the Laodiceans some indication that a longer church letter was being sent to Colossae and would reach them in due time?

3. Tychicus is not mentioned in Philemon. This would be natural if Colossians (where he is fully introduced and authenticated) and Philemon were addressed ultimately to the same church, but it calls for some explanation if Philemon is a letter to the Laodicean church.

4. The otherwise strange return to the singular number in Philem. 23 (ἀσπάζεταί σε Ἐπαφρᾶς . . .) is readily understandable on the assumption that Philemon was addressed to Colossae, because in Colossians the members

49

of the church as a whole have been greeted by Paul's associates at the time. But if this letter is addressed to a church in a different city, the apparently deliberate choice of the singular σε is less naturally explicable.

5. Paul represents Onesimus as arriving at Colossae (Col. 4:7-9), but what assurance of that fact would he have had if Onesimus' owner lived in Laodicea and Philemon was addressed there? A glance at the map of Asia Minor will suggest what a study of the roads will confirm[12]—that it is extremely unlikely that Paul's messengers reached Colossae except by way of Laodicea. Unless they came into the Lycus valley from the East, which is very improbable,[13] they would normally have passed through Laodicea on their way to Colossae. But can we actually picture Onesimus continuing through or barely skirting that city, if his master lived there, to visit Colossae with Tychicus before returning to Laodicea to interview his owner?

6. In this same paragraph of Colossians (4:7-9) Paul explains why he is sending Tychicus, but gives no explanation of Onesimus' coming. He merely writes that he is sending Tychicus "with Onesimus," as though the reason for the latter's coming was obvious enough. But does this not suggest that Onesimus belonged in Colossae, as well as the fact that the other letter in which Onesimus' case was dealt with was being sent there?

[12] E.g., W. M. Ramsay, *The Cities and Bishoprics of Phrygia* (Oxford, 1895), or *Historical Geography of Asia Minor* (London, 1890).

[13] The view, never widely held, that Paul may have written Philemon and Colossians from Caesarea is now usually rejected. But see Lohmeyer, *op. cit.*, p. 15, where this view is defended.

7. But the really important consideration is yet to be mentioned. Here, as at every other point, it is the relation of this letter to Colossians which is decisive. If, as we have seen, Colossians is very much concerned with what happens to Onesimus, one would surely expect it to be addressed to the community where Onesimus and his master lived. If they lived in Laodicea, why was "Colossians" not sent there? In that case, why was this letter, intended for the Laodiceans as well as the Colossians (4:16), not directed to Laodicea in the first instance, especially since, as we have noted, it very probably passed through that city on its way?

In fact, the longer one considers the matter of the relative importance of Laodicea and Colossae, both as cities and as churches, the more pertinent seems the inquiry as to how it happens that there is a letter of Paul to the Colossians at all. Not only was Colossae very near the other city; it was at this period insignificant beside it. Lightfoot writes:

Asia Minor under the Romans was divided into districts, each comprising several towns and having its chief city, in which the courts were held from time to time by the proconsul or legate of the province, and where the taxes from the subordinate towns were collected. . . . At the head of the most important of these political dioceses, the "Cibyratic convention" or "jurisdiction," as it was called, comprising not less than twenty-five towns, stood Laodicea. Here in times past Cicero, as proconsul of Cilicia, had held his court; hither at stated seasons flocked suitors, advocates, clerks, sheriffs'-officers, tax-collectors, pleasure-seekers, courtiers—all those crowds whom business or leisure or policy or curiosity would draw together from a wealthy and populous district, when the representative of the laws and the majesty of Rome appeared to receive homage and to hold his assize. To this position as the chief city of the Cibyratic union the inscriptions probably refer, when they style Laodicea the "metropolis." And in its metropolitan rank we see an explanation of the fact, that to Laodicea as the center of a Christian diocese also, whence their letters would readily be circulated among the neighboring brotherhoods, two apostles addressed themselves in succession, the one writing from his captivity in Rome, the other from his exile at Patmos.[14]

The last reference, needless to say, is to the book of Revelation, which includes among the letters to the seven churches of Asia a letter to the church at Laodicea. But although it may be said that the other "apostle," Paul, also sent a letter to the Laodiceans (viz., our Colossians), it was to be read first at Colossae, a fact which calls for explanation.

For Colossae seems to have been as unimportant as Laodicea was conspicuous and influential. Its earlier glory had passed. To quote Lightfoot again:

Strabo, writing about two generations before St. Paul, describes it as a "small town" in the district of which Laodicea was the capital. We shall therefore be prepared to find that, while Laodicea and Hierapolis both hold important places in the early records of the Church, Colossae disappears wholly

[14] J. B. Lightfoot, *St. Paul's Epistles to the Colossians and to Philemon* (London: Macmillan and Company, 1886), pp. 7-8. See also Ramsay, *The Cities and Bishoprics of Phrygia.*

from the pages of history. Its comparative insignificance is still attested by its ruins, which are few and meagre, while the vast remains of temples, baths, theatres, aqueducts, gymnasia, and sepulchres, strewing the extensive sites of its more fortunate neighbors, still bear witness to their ancient prosperity and magnificence. It is not even mentioned by Ptolemy, though his enumeration of towns includes several inconsiderable places. Without doubt Colossae was the least important church to which any epistle of St. Paul is addressed.[15]

This fact, to which no one will take exception, is the more striking because of the great importance and near proximity of Laodicea. Why, we repeat, is a letter intended for both Laodicea and Colossae, sent first to Colossae?

No one will be inclined to urge that there was some religious condition or theological problem at Colossae which did not also exist in the neighboring church. Are we not forced to conclude that some personal reason accounts for the first address of Colossians? And what could this personal reason be unless it had some connection with Onesimus? We are far from asserting that the only reason Paul wrote Colossians was to forward his plans about Onesimus; we are suggesting that this was most probably why he sent the letter first to Colossae. He has just made a very considerable request of a member of the Colossian church, whom in all likelihood he does not know (Philem. 4). Certainly he does not know the church (Col. 1:4; 2:1), but he is eager that the congregation shall support him in his Christian demands upon one of its members.

[15] Lightfoot, *op. cit.*, p. 16.

He writes a longer letter to the church as a whole, therefore, a part of the purpose of which was surely to establish between himself and them the cordial relation which will assure their co-operation in securing the kind of action on the part of one of their number which he very earnestly desires. In this letter he discusses various matters of common interest and importance among the churches of the Lycus valley, about which he would perhaps in any case have written them, but his sending this communication first to Colossae was due, we believe, to the residence there of the household to which Onesimus belonged.

But, after all, we do not need to establish so much in order to show the probability of a Colossian destination for Philemon. We need only ask if any consideration can explain Paul's writing and sending such a letter as our Colossians to Colossae (with the request that it be sent back, or on, to Laodicea) if the other letter, which it so decisively supported and which so critically needed its support, went with Onesimus to Laodicea.

From all of this two probabilities have emerged, each of them very strong indeed: first, that the destination of Philemon was Colossae; and, second, that when Paul directs the Colossians in another letter to read the "letter from Laodicea," he is referring to our Philemon. To assume that both cannot be true is quite gratuitous. To accept as likely the identity of Philemon with the "letter from Laodicea" by no means involves one in the conclusion that Philemon was sent to Laodiceans. As a matter of fact, it is the quite unnecessary identification of the "letter from Laodicea" with a "Laodiceans" and the consequent necessity of establishing a Laodicean destination for Philemon, which has often weakened an otherwise strong position. Something in the manner of transmission of Philemon must account for Paul's description of it. It was to reach Colossae "from Laodicea." I shall later make a more specific, even if very tentative, suggestion at this point.[16]

We thus see that Philemon and Colossians are related to each other in the closest possible fashion. The occasion of Philemon, if not also the occasion of Colossians, at any rate accounts for much of its content and very probably for its particular church address. Colossians was written at the same time as Philemon, sent by the same messengers, to the same community; but even more than that—it actually alludes to the other letter and urges its readers to read it also. The correlation may appear complete, but there is yet another remarkable point of contact between the two letters, the meaning of which we must now explore.

[16] C. F. D. Moule (*op. cit.,* p. 18), in rejecting the proposed identification of the "letter from Laodicea," writes: "Col. iv. 16 requires to be rather severely strained to fit [it]; for what is contemplated in that verse is manifestly an *exchange* of letters." This is "manifestly" true only if one begins by assuming that Paul actually wrote a letter at this time to the Laodicean church. But this is an assumption: the language of Col. 4:16 does not require it, and there is absolutely no evidence for the existence of such a letter. Let us suppose that we were in the position of knowing definitely that Paul did in fact send two letters which were eventually to reach Colossae but one of which was to arrive by way of Laodicea—in that case, would not Col. 4:16 have to be "rather severely strained" to support the sense which may now appear as the only natural one? Moule concludes his discussion of the verse with a good question (p. 139) : "But why, then [on the assumption that there was a letter to the Laodicean church], does Paul address messages to Laodicean Christians in this letter to Colossae?"

CHAPTER III

————————

Philemon and Archippus

I

THE CONNECTION OF ARCHIPPUS WITH BOTH COLOSSIANS AND
Philemon has been mentioned more than once. He is
named, as Onesimus is also, in both letters. He is one of
the addressees of Philemon and is mentioned in Colossians
in such a way as to suggest some connection between him
and the "letter from Laodicea." What is that connection?
Why does Paul after writing to the Colossian Christians,
καὶ τὴν ἐκ Λαοδικίας [ποιήσατε] ἵνα καὶ ὑμεῖς ἀναγνῶτε continue immediately with καὶ εἴπατε Ἀρχίππῳ, βλέπε τὴν
διακονίαν ἣν παρέλαβες ἐν κυρίῳ, ἵνα αὐτὴν πληροῖς Col. 4:16-
17)?

It is our judgment that Paul's statement here indicates a
connection not only between the "letter from Laodicea"
and Archippus but also between this letter and the διακονία
which Archippus must discharge. In other words, the
"letter from Laodicea" must either explicitly or by implication have laid upon Archippus some religious obligation
which Paul here requests the Colossian church to en-

courage him to fulfill. This correlation between the ἐπιστολήν and the διακονίαν is indicated not only by the obviously close connection of the two sentences but also by the resemblance in form of the sentences themselves, both involving an imperative and a ἵνα-clause. Whatever may be the fact, there can be little doubt that the most natural reading of Col. 4:16-17 would suggest at once that the letter imposed the obligation. If we should read Colossians first and had the "letter from Laodicea" at hand, we should turn to it with every expectation of finding Archippus' "service" described there or at least alluded to. But we *do* have this letter at hand in our Philemon, and when having turned to it, we discover at once that it is actually addressed to Archippus among others, our expectation is enormously strengthened. This expectation, moreover, does not depend upon the identification of Philemon with "the letter from Laodicea." For Philemon, whether it was this letter or not, is known to have been written at the same time as Colossians and was certainly addressed among others to Archippus. We cannot avoid asking, therefore, whether it is likely that Paul will fail to mention in this letter addressed to Archippus himself a duty of his, of which in another letter written at the same time he urges the Colossian church to remind him? The conclusion seems irresistible that somewhere in Philemon reference is made to Archippus' διακονία.

But where in so brief a letter can this reference be hidden? We read Philemon again and are startled by a really remarkable fact: The entire letter is concerned with a διακονία. A slaveowner is asked to give up a slave for

Christian service. A study of Paul's usage will show that no word would have served so admirably to designate the obligation under which he was placing Onesimus' master.[1] He even uses the verb διακονέω in describing the service which Onesimus is to render *in his master's place* (ἵνα ὑπὲρ σοῦ μοι διακονῇ ἐν τοῖς δεσμοῖς τοῦ εὐαγγελίου).[2] But this clearly points to Archippus' being the owner of the slave, whereas that person was Philemon. But was he? Although it is not a matter upon which I am inclined to insist, I suggest that all of the difficulties in the complex Philemon-Colossians relationship can best be met by the assumption that Archippus was the owner. That this assumption is by no means impossible I believe the examination of the first paragraph of the letter will show.

II

This opening paragraph of address and greeting is as follows:

Παῦλος δέσμιος Χριστοῦ Ἰησοῦ καὶ Τιμόθεος ὁ ἀδαλφὸς Φιλήμονι τῷ ἀγαπητῷ καὶ συνεργῷ ἡμῶν καὶ Ἀπφίᾳ τῇ ἀδελφῇ καὶ Ἀρχίππῳ τῷ συστρατιώτῃ ἡμῶν καὶ τῇ κατ' οἶκόν σου ἐκκλησίᾳ. Χάρις ὑμῖν καὶ εἰρήνη ἀπὸ θεοῦ πατρὸς ἡμῶν καὶ κυρίου Ἰησοῦ Χριστοῦ.

[1] It is interesting to recall in this connection the sentence of Jülicher which has already been quoted (above, p. 30), "It seems that he expected the liberation of the slave as the one *service* (*Dienst*) to which, for the sake of the Gospel, he laid claim." Lohmeyer uses the same word (*Die Briefe an die Kolosser und an Philemon*, p. 191). Moule's objection (*op. cit.*, p. 16) that the word for "received" (παρέλαβες) "is better suited to something 'handed on,' as by tradition" does not seem to me serious; surely the verb was used in many connections.

[2] Also cf. ἐν κυρίῳ in Col. 4:17 with the same phrase in Philem. 20.

It will be noticed that the letter is sent to three individuals and a church which met in the house of one of them. But although in the greeting and in the concluding sentences of the epistle all of these persons apparently are addressed, since the plural pronoun of the second person is used, the body of the letter—the part which deals with the case of Onesimus—is written quite in the style of a private communication, the pronoun of the second person being consistently singular. This person, the owner of Onesimus, is, we may be sure, one of the individuals named in the salutation, but as to which one the literary facts give us no right to the same measure of certainty.

It may be argued that since Philemon is named first among the recipients of the note, he must have been the slave's master. So it has always been assumed. And if this were an ordinary letter, we should agree without hesitation. But the fact is that it is far from being an ordinary letter.[3] A rather extensive search through papyri and other ancient letters has failed to disclose anything even remotely resembling it in form. It was a letter to a church, embodying (would we say, "inclosing"?) a letter to an individual and involves a curious combination of the characteristics of both types which may well place it in a class of its own. Described more exactly, it is an epistle to a church, addressed also specifically to certain individuals and containing a particular message for one of them, in which the others, however, were felt to be concerned. Put in yet an-

[3] "A surprising mixture of the singular and plural both in the persons speaking and in the persons addressed . . . points at once to some peculiarity in the composition of the epistle" (van Manen, "The Epistle to Philemon").

other way, it is a letter to an individual, the reading of which, it was desired, should be "overheard" by a group to which the individual belonged and which was able to exercise some control over his conduct. It is, then, an altogether extraordinary letter and we may easily take too much for granted about it. We have no right to assume that merely because Philemon is greeted first in a letter which especially concerned Onesimus' master, he must have been that individual. In the absence of other evidence, that would undoubtedly be most probable, but even so, it would be by no means certain. Paul has already violated ordinary letter practice in letting so many people "in" on what soon has the form of a private note. We cannot be sure that he did not further violate it in the order in which he names these other persons. He has reasons, to be sure, for including them—he wants the whole church community to know (cf. Col. 4:16) what he is asking of Onesimus' master. He wants their help in guaranteeing to Onesimus a friendly reception and in securing him for his own service. But as there plainly would have been reasons for naming Philemon quite apart from any legal connection he may have sustained with Onesimus, so there may have been reasons for naming him first. To mention the most likely—this "dear fellow-worker" may have been the official leader of the church which is to be the ultimate executor and custodian of the letter. If Philemon is in any real sense a church letter, dealing as we have seen with a church matter, would there not have been every reason for naming the responsible leader of the church first?

That the person first named in the salutation of a letter

is not necessarily the individual with whom the writer is
to be most concerned is probably obvious enough, but
it may be useful to refer to a papyrus letter of the fourth or
fifth century, P. Giss., I, Nr. 54. It is addressed to two
individuals, as follows:

κυρί[ῳ] μου τιμιωτάτῳ ἀδελφῷ Ὀλυμπιοδώρῳ
καὶ Ἑρμαείωνι.[4]

After a short sentence intended for both, in which the
pronoun of the second person is plural, the writer turns to
Hermaeion, named second in the salutation and addresses
the larger part of the letter to him, using the singular
number. After giving certain directions to this individual,
toward the close of the communication the writer says to
his other addressee, "And help him in every way, most
worthy Olympiodorus," but seems almost at once to return
to Hermaeion with a final word of instruction, although
it should be said that one cannot be quite sure who is
being addressed at this last point. The letter closes with
some remarks and greetings for both. This note is interesting as involving a mixture of singular and plural pronouns
not unlike that found in Philemon. It is particularly relevant to our discussion, however, because the person named
first in the address is evidently not the individual with
whom the writer is most immediately concerned. It may be
added that the reason this person was named first may well

[4] E. Kornemann and P. M. Meyer, *Griechishe Papyri zu Giessen* (Leipzig
and Berlin, 1910-12). The address may be translated: "To my most honored
lord and brother Olympiodorus and to Hermaeion."

be that he was for the writer the more important individual. At the beginning he is called κύριος μου τιμιώτατος
ἀδελφὸς Ὀλυμπιόδωρος and when he is addressed in the
body of the note it is again as τιμιώτατε Ὀλυμπιόδωρε. Some
such consideration would naturally account for Philemon's
being named first in Paul's letter.

As a matter of fact, there is only one phrase in the salutation of Philemon which explicitly identifies the owner of
the slave, and that phrase unfortunately is one whose
meaning for us must be equivocal—although it is important to remember that it was not so for the first readers.
It is the phrase "and the church that meets in *your* house."
In his first paragraph it was only in the singular pronoun
"your" (σου) that Paul designated beyond question the
individual in the church addressed with whom he was to
be most concerned. For the original readers that was
enough, since they knew in whose house the church met,
but *we* can only surmise. Does the "your" refer to Philemon or is it to be taken with Archippus, who is named
immediately before it? I suggest that if it were not for the
apparent force of the primacy of Philemon's name in the
letter, we should naturally associate the church with
Archippus' house. I am convinced that even when the
priority of Philemon's name is given its due weight, there
are additional facts which justify us in at least proposing
that Archippus, the person named nearest this decisive
phrase, τῇ κατ᾽ οἶκόν σου ἐκκλησίᾳ was the owner of both
house and slave, and that it was to him that Paul directed
the body of his letter. I should like to name the considerations which have led to this conclusion.

62

III

The first of these grows out of the effort actually to visualize the situation Paul and Onesimus faced as they looked toward Colossae. According to the ordinary view, Onesimus has run away from his master and quite possibly has robbed him. He has thus laid himself open to any penalty his master might be disposed to lay on him. Paul decides that he should return to Colossae, but is determined that no harm shall come to him. Whether this view is altogether correct or not, there can be little doubt of an additional fact—Paul wants Onesimus to be sent back. To help assure this very earnestly desired result he writes a letter which Onesimus is to take with him. But Paul is troubled because he does not know Onesimus' master. He finds himself critically dependent upon the will of someone whom he cannot fully trust to comply with his desires. What, then, will he do? He will address his letter not to the slave-master only but to a church, which happened to meet in his house. But what assurance will he have that the church will actually receive the letter? He guarantees this in some measure by informing the Colossians (Col. 4:16) of the note and directing them to read it. But may he not naturally do more than this? If Paul is eager that the whole Christian community shall know of his plan, will he not direct his letter first to some disinterested and firmly trusted friend, and only then to the slaveowner himself? If this friend was the recognized leader of the church which is to read the letter, this procedure would have seemed quite normal to all who were concerned.

It may be objected that the cordial tone of the note indicates personal acquaintance between Paul and the slaveowner. It must not be overlooked, however, that Paul had everything to gain by adopting this tone; Colossians, certainly addressed to a personally unknown group, is written in the same spirit, perhaps for the same reason. Paul begins his message to the slaveowner, *"I have heard* of your love." He knows that "the hearts of the saints have been refreshed" by this "brother." And when later he pleads, "Refresh *my* heart," the suggestion is strong that he had not himself previously been the beneficiary of his reader's generosity. Needless to say, the fact that Paul regarded the slaveowner as in his debt, apparently because he was a Christian, would not in any degree warrant the conclusion that Paul had directly influenced him. Paul in Colossians (1:7-8) virtually claims as his own the work which Epaphras has done in Colossae. That Paul had a lively sense of his authority and proprietorship among the churches founded even indirectly under his influence there is quite enough evidence in his letters to demonstrate.

But whether Paul had actually met the slaveowner or not, he clearly did not have the implicit confidence in his obedience which for good tactical reasons he gladly claims (Philem. 23). If so, why so much concern in Colossians with Onesimus' case and the earnest direction that its readers should also read Philemon? What more natural, then, than that he should direct that letter first to someone of whom he had more complete knowledge and in whom he felt quite unreserved confidence?

This somewhat a priori judgment is confirmed in some

measure, I believe, by the manner in which Paul describes the two principal addressees of his note. Philemon is his "dear fellow-worker"; Archippus is his "fellow-soldier." Now whether it is possible to determine the significance for Paul of these two terms is certainly open to question, but we need not hesitate to assert that they had significance. It is doubtful that there is a chance word in the epistle; we may feel quite sure that Paul did not just happen to designate our two persons in exactly the way he does. Ἀδελφή may be a general and fairly colorless word;[5] not so, συνεργός and συνστρατιώτης. It may be worth while to inquire, therefore, whether it was to the "fellow-worker" or to the "fellow-soldier" that Paul was the more probably looking for the release of Onesimus.

The term συνεργός Paul applies in the course of his letters to the following individuals: Prisca and Aquila (Rom. 16:3), Urbanus (Rom. 16:9), Timothy (Rom. 16:21 and I Thess. 3:2), Titus (II Cor. 8:23), Epaphroditus (Phil. 2:25), Clement (Phil. 4:3), and (in Colossians and Philemon) to Epaphras, Aristarchus, Jesus Justus, Mark, Demas, Luke, and Philemon. Of these fourteen individuals, it is certain that six (Prisca, Aquila, Timothy, Titus, Mark, and Epaphras) were active sharers with Paul in the work of spreading his message and supervising his churches. That Luke, Demas, Jesus Justus, and Aristarchus were also actual associates of Paul—real fellow-workers—

---

[5] That Apphia was the wife of Philemon has usually been regarded as probable. It is possible that she was the wife of Archippus. There is, needless to say, nothing to require the opinion that she was the wife of either.

would seem to be indicated by his manner of reference in each case. Of Urbanus we know nothing. In connection with Clement, reference is made to "the rest of my fellow-workers" and they are described as working at my side (συνήθλησαν) in spreading the gospel." Of Epaphroditus we know that he was of assistance to Paul during the imprisonment in which Philippians was written, and he is said to have been near death because of the "Lord's work" (ἔργον). All of this would indicate that the term συνεργός meant usually, if not invariably, an actual and active personal participation in Paul's activity. It was likewise, one would gather, a term of great regard, reserved apparently for those who have been also Paul's "fellow-prisoners," who have "risked their necks" for him, who "have worked at his side," etc. Luke, who in one instance is referred to as συνεργός, in the other is described as ἀγαπητός. Only once are the words συνεργός and ἀγαπητός used together, and that is in characterizing Philemon. I submit that this fact, in view of Paul's usage, would strongly indicate that Philemon was the object of Paul's warm regard and was an associate of his in the work of Christian preaching and administration. But Onesimus' owner Paul evidently did not know, and there is every suggestion that he sustained with him no such relation as the term συνεργός would seem to have connoted. As a matter of fact, a close reading of the letter will indicate that the slaveowner was more probably a benefactor of the church than an active laborer in it. It would appear that if Philemon is the individual to whom Paul is appealing through the church, he is using the terms in which he describes him very loosely indeed. If, on the other hand, Philemon was the overseer of the churches in the valley of the Lycus, as Epaphras apparently had formerly been, and therefore of the church to which the letter is addressed, he is described in exactly the terms we should expect.

The word συνστρατιώτης (fellow soldier), used of Archippus, is found in Paul only once besides—Ἐπαφρόδιτον . . . συνστρατιώτην μου, ὑμῶν δὲ ἀπόστολον καὶ λειτουργὸν τῆς χρείας μου (Phil. 2:25). Because of the comparative rarity of the word, not only in Paul but also in the general literature of the period (it occurs apparently only once in Josephus and hardly more than a half-dozen times in the published papyri), it is doubtless impossible to determine its meaning with any assurance. It may well be accidental that in the only two letters of Paul in which a financial partnership between himself and another and business accounts are alluded to—Philippians and Philemon—the word συνστρατιώτης occurs. But if it is altogether accidental, it is indeed strange that its rare occurrences in the papyri also seem generally to have connection with some business or money transaction. Moulton and Milligan [6] cite the case of a boy who writes his mother that he has borrowed money from a "fellow-soldier": κέχρημαι χαλκὸν π[α]ρὰ συστρατιώτου (BGU, III, 814 [third century]). [7] In a papyrus letter of the same or somewhat earlier period the following appears: ἥνικα ἐστρατευόμην, . . . παρεθέμην Πετεσούχῳ τινὶ συνστρατ[ιώτ]ῃ μου καὶ φίλῳ σκεύη ἐν συντιμήσει

[6] *The Vocabulary of the Greek New Testament, s. v.*

[7] *Ägyptische Urkunden aus den königlichen Museen zu Berlin: Griechische Urkunden,* Vol. III (Berlin, 1903).

δραχμῶν ὀκτακοσίων (BGU, I, 4).[8] In P. Meyer, 20 the word συνστρατιώτης occurs with a closely related connotation: ἔπεμψα διὰ Διοσκόρ[ο]υ συνστρατιώτου . . . δηνάρια τ[ρι]άκοντα.[9] One can hardly help recalling in connection with this sentence the fact that Epaphroditus, Paul's "fellow soldier," had been sent with money for his use. The phrase, "friend and fellow-soldier," noted in BGU, I, 4, quoted above, is all but duplicated in P. Goodspeed, Chicago, II, iii: φίλον καὶ σύμμαχον ὄντα.[10] The total number of instances is too small to justify a generalization, but surely it appears more than possible that the term συνστρατιώτης was used, as our word "comrade," to designate a helper in time of need, an ally, a befriender. So it seems to have been employed by Josephus, who tells us that Fortune must have been Titus' helper (συστρατιῶτις) at the siege of Jerusalem.[11]

If such was the frequent meaning of the term, I suggest that it fits the owner of Onesimus, as his character and function in the Christian community at Colossae emerge in the rest of the letter, better than συνεργός, and particularly that it fits the request Paul is going to make of him. This Christian who cannot labor himself is asked to give

[8] *Ibid.*, Vol. I (Berlin, 1895). Translation: "When I was in the army, . . . I gave Petesouchus, a fellow soldier and friend of mine, stores having a value of 800 drachmas."

[9] "I have sent through Dioscorus, a fellow soldier . . . 30 denarii." P. M. Meyer, *Griechische Texte aus Ägypten* (Berlin, 1916).

[10] E. J. Goodspeed, *Chicago Literary Papyri* (Chicago, 1908). It is interesting to note that both Liddell and Scott and Bauer recognize that σύμμαχος, an obvious synonym of συνστρατιώτης, had even in classical times come to mean "helper" in a general, nonmilitary, sense.

[11] *Bell. Jud.* VI. 9. 1.

Onesimus to serve in his place. That may well have seemed the rôle of a "fellow-soldier." It is very striking that in the Philippians passage (2:25) Epaphroditus is called "my fellow-soldier . . . and minister to my need."

But the really important argument lies in the final paragraph of Colossians. Why is our letter, Philemon, not identified there more fully? The letter itself is referred to as "from Laodicea"; Onesimus is named in it; does one not expect to hear somewhere in that letter the name of Onesimus' master? Would not Paul have identified the "letter from Laodicea" further, this time unmistakably, by naming the second individual principally concerned in it? We have seen that Paul in his anxiety about Onesimus has gradually led up to the injunction that the Colossians are to read our Philemon. But he is still not content. "Read the letter from Laodicea," he concludes, "and say to Archippus, 'See that you fulfil the διακονία you have received!'" What was this διακονία of Archippus? In the light of all the facts is not the answer logically almost inevitable? He was Onesimus' master; through Philemon and the church, he is asked to give him up for Paul's service. Thus and thus only does this important sentence at the very end of Colossians become not only intelligible but luminous.

One additional consideration may be noted. It will be recalled that in the preceding chapter we found ourselves forced to identify our Philemon with the letter referred to in Col. 4:16 as "from Laodicea," and yet compelled also to affirm the Colossian residence of Onesimus and his master. It was pointed out that there is no essential contradition between these two statements, and that any number of possible facts about the manner of transmission or delivery of the letter might account for Paul's way of describing it. It is possible now to make a more specific, even if very tentative, suggestion—Philemon may well have been a Laodicean. In fact, if he was the "fellow-worker" we have described, to whom the church at Colossae would look for leadership, Laodicea would have been his natural place of residence, for it was, no doubt, the center from which the evangelization of the Lycus valley was supervised. But if this was true and the note was first of all delivered to Philemon, who was expected to see that it and Onesimus reached Archippus and the Colossian church under his patronage, Paul might well allude to it in another letter written simultaneously and sent directly to Colossae as "the letter from Laodicea."

With that allusion and the reference to Archippus' διακονία, Colossians proper ends. Paul then takes the stylus to write the final words. It is not an accident that he writes, μνημονεύετέ μου τῶν δεσμῶν. Five times in Philemon he has reminded his readers that he is a prisoner for the good news. It is the basis upon which in considerable part he has made his appeal for Onesimus. Now in Colossians he follows his references to that letter and to Archippus with another reminder. It is Paul, "the ambassador in chains" (Eph. 6:20), who has asked for Onesimus. Will Archippus be disposed to deny such a request? Will the church at Colossae be willing to allow him to do so?

CHAPTER IV

———•—•———

Philemon and the Pauline Letter Collection

I

THE HISTORY OF THE LETTERS OF PAUL FROM THE TIME OF their writing until near the end of the first century of our era is very obscure. That they remained completely buried and unused in the chests of the several churches would appear on a priori grounds to be unlikely. Paul had been too important in the establishment of these churches in Greece and Asia Minor and had been too significant in the controversy with the Judaizers, who threatened at one time to divide the church, for his letters not to have enjoyed, in some quarters at least, devoted (if not partisan) use from the beginning. That during this period, however, they circulated very far from the churches to which they were severally addressed seems questionable, although there can be little doubt that one church might have a number of letters. The fact that Mark, Matthew, and Luke-Acts, the only extant Christian books which can with any degree of plausibility be regarded as having their

71

origin in this period, do not show the influence of Paul's letters is very striking, although it may well be that a gospel in any case could not have been a characteristic product of Paulinism. The epistles, however, were such a product, and would serve to nourish, in some measure at least, Pauline churches and Pauline Christians from the start.

That Paulinism did not die, the Paulinist Marcion who came to Rome from Asia Minor about A.D. 140 is sufficient evidence. We may be sure that he represents a tradition (however extreme or erratic may have been his own protagonism of it) which goes back to Paul himself, a tradition of which Paul's letters must always have been a part. And as it was Marcion who seems first to have canonized the Pauline epistles, it must have been the movement within Christianity, of which Marcion was largely the product, which at an earlier stage preserved them. Or to approach the same point from the earlier side—as it was Paul who wrote the letters, so, we may be sure, it was Pauline churches which cherished them and at some time toward the end of the century published as a formal and authorized collection the ten epistles (including Ephesians) which we now possess.

That such a publication took place, Goodspeed has, in the judgment of many, abundantly demonstrated.[1] The

---

[1] E. J. Goodspeed, *New Solutions of New Testament Problems* (Chicago, 1927), pp. 1-64; *The Meaning of Ephesians* (Chicago, 1933); and *The Formation of the New Testament* (Chicago, 1926), pp. 20 ff.; *An Introduction to the New Testament* (Chicago, 1937), pp. viii ff.; 210 ff.; and other writings. See also on this subject, T. Zahn, *Geschichte des Neutestamentlichen Kanons* (Erlangen: A. Deichert, 1888), I, 262-302; II, 58-88; A.

striking fact that the book of Revelation begins with a corpus of letters to churches—if indeed, as Martin Rist [2] suggests, that book as a whole (that is, after 1:3) should not be thought of as being an apocalypse in letter form—and indeed that other letters begin with apparent suddenness to be written all over Christendom is itself almost sufficient proof. The Epistle to the Hebrews, I Clement, and perhaps I Peter (certainly no earlier date for this letter is possible) all appear, as does Revelation, in the last decade of the first century, and early in the next we have the church letters of Ignatius (also a corpus). The Epistle of Polycarp to the Philippians, not to mention the letters of John, James, Jude, the Pastorals, II Peter, and other letters soon followed. In some of these cases, it is true, the "letter" may originally have been an essay or homily. But the fact that such a writing came almost at once to be regarded as a letter or was put, in whole or part, into epistolary form only makes the point more clear. The apparently sudden adoption of the letter-form

Harnack, *Die Briefsammlung des Apostels Paulus und die andern vorkonstantinishen Christlichen Briefsammlungen* (Leipzig: J. C. Hinnichs, 1926) ; P. N. Harrison, *Polycarp's Two Epistles to the Philippians* (Cambridge: University Press, 1936), pp 231-310; Lucetta Mowry, "The Early Circulation of Paul's Letters," *Journal of Biblical Literature*, LXIII, Part II (1944) 73 ff.; C. L. Mitton, *The Formation of the Pauline Letter Corpus* (London: Epworth Press, 1955) ; G. Zuntz, *The Text of the Epistles: A Disquisition upon the Corpus Paulinum* (London: Oxford University Press, 1946) . I should also like to call attention to my own *Marcion and the New Testament* (Chicago: University of Chicago Press, 1942), pp. 39-76, 172-76, where a fuller statement can be found on many of the matters dealt with in this chapter. A few paragraphs from that book, now out of print, have been incorporated in this; but for the most part that discussion is independent and supplementary.

[2] *The Interpreter's Bible,* Vol. XII, p. 550.

as the medium of Christian teaching can be accounted for most naturally by the assumption that near the end of the first century the letters of Paul, which had severally enjoyed a limited circulation in the churches of Asia Minor and Greece, were published more widely and as a formal and authoritative corpus.

This supposition, as Goodspeed shows, is confirmed when we examine the contents of the various letters and letter collections just mentioned, because they show so generally the influence of Paul's thought and style. I Peter clearly exhibits knowledge of the Pauline letters, notably of Romans and Ephesians. The letters of Revelation are introduced by the characteristic Pauline benediction of "grace to you and peace" (χάρις ὑμῖν καὶ εἰρήνη). The author of I Clement, the letter sent by the church at Rome to the church at Corinth about A.D. 95, writes, "Take up the letter of the blessed Paul the apostle. What was the first thing he wrote you in the beginning of the gospel (ἐν ἀρχῇ τοῦ εὐαγγελίου)?" In answering his question he shows undoubted acquaintance with a section of our I Corinthians. It is clear also that Clement knew Romans and Ephesians and very likely that he had read our II Corinthians. And I cannot help seeing in the rather strange phrase "in the beginning of the gospel" a better than possible reminiscence of Phil. 4:14, its only other occurrence in New Testament, Apostolic Fathers, or Apologists.

The large use of Philemon by Ignatius we shall notice later. There is ample ground for attributing to him also knowledge of Romans, I Corinthians, Galatians, Philippians, and Ephesians. Ignatius makes an explicit reference to Paul (one of two in all of his letters) in Eph. 12, telling his readers that in "every letter" (πάσῃ ἐπιστολῇ), Paul remembers them. Polycarp in his Philippians twice alludes to Paul's letters and shows the influence of Romans, I and II Corinthians, Galatians, II Thessalonians, Ephesians, and, I believe, Philippians.[3]

It will have been noticed that to all of these writers who show the influence of Paul's letters, Ephesians seems also to have been known. This is striking in view of the likelihood, already noted, that Ephesians was not the work of Paul at all but was composed a generation after his death. This universal acquaintance with Ephesians among those who know any of the Pauline epistles suggests that Ephesians must have appeared with these epistles when they were published. And when one finds that Ephesians is based upon the particular nine epistles of Paul which we have and upon nothing else except the author-editor's very considerable ability to rework and reorder the Pauline materials the probability that Ephesians was written on the occasion of the publication becomes stronger.[4] Since it appears not to have been addressed to any particular church, but to the church in its corporate, universal aspect, it would have served admirably to in-

[3] For a comprehensive study of the use of Paul's letters by later writers in the early period see A. E. Barnett, *Paul Becomes a Literary Influence* (Chicago: University of Chicago Press, 1941) .

[4] Goodspeed devotes pp. 79-165 of his *The Meaning of Ephesians* (Chicago: University of Chicago Press, 1933) , to demonstrating the fact here stated. His conclusions are in all essential respects confirmed by C. L. Mitton's independent investigation in *The Epistle to the Ephesians* (*op. cit.*) . See also Goodspeed's later book, *The Key to Ephesians* (Chicago, 1956) , pp. 2-73.

troduce the collection. Any number of internal facts, which Goodspeed has adduced, confirm the supposition that this was its purpose and function. And when it is observed that the messages to the several churches in Revelation are preceded by a message addressed to them all together, the case becomes strong indeed.

In this early collection Philemon had a place. I believe that the evidence will permit us to be more specific and to indicate exactly what this place was. This evidence lies chiefly in the earliest list of Paul's letters of which we have definite record, that of Marcion, the importance of whose influence upon the subsequent development of the New Testament canon has many times been explored, but whose importance as a mirror in which earlier stages of that development are reflected has not, perhaps, been adequately recognized. A comprehensive study of Marcion from this point of view would, I feel sure, prove very rewarding. The present inquiry into the implications of Marcion's letter list is but the beginning of such a study.[5]

II

The sources of our knowledge of Marcion's canon of Paul's letters are largely Tertullian and Epiphanius, both of whom denounced vigorously and at some length the heretical movement which Marcion was charged with initiating. Both writers agree in their account of the contents of Marcion's ἀποστολικόν. It contained the ten letters,

[5] That study was taken at least a little bit further in my *Marcion and the New Testament,* published seven years after the first edition of this book.

Romans, I and II Corinthians, Galatians, Ephesians, Philippians, Colossians, I and II Thessalonians, and Philemon. As to the order in which these epistles were arranged in Marcion's list our two authorities agree except at one point. In order to present the facts in the clearest possible way, we shall tentatively assume the accuracy of Tertullian's account and discuss its implications, after which we shall be in better position to evaluate the significance of Epiphanius' divergence.

According to Tertullian, then, the list of Marcion seems to have contained the letters of Paul in the following order:[6] Galatians, I Corinthians, II Corinthians, Romans, I Thessalonians, II Thessalonians, Ephesians (called by Marcion, Laodiceans), Colossians, Philippians, Philemon.

This is the earliest list we have and dates, as we have intimated, from the middle of the second century, not more than fifty years after the first publication of the Pauline collection. It contains the same ten letters. Would we not expect that it should contain them in the same order? Why should the order have changed materially in the half-century, or is there any reason to suspect that Marcion himself would alter the arrangement in any thoroughgoing way? And, as a mater of fact, an examination of his list does not suggest that he has done so, except at one point—Galatians has first place and in view of the peculiarly vigorous anti-Judaism of this epistle, it is fair to surmise that its primacy is due to Marcion's own preference for it. But is it not likely that except for this quite

6 *Adv. Marcion. v.*

characteristic variation, the order of Marcion's list was the original one?

This appears the more probable when we observe that the arrangement is by no means haphazard. It is, generally speaking, the order of length.[7] This fact has been usually overlooked because the Corinthian and the Thessalonian letters have for many centuries been considered as four separate epistles, rather than, as they were undoubtedly at first regarded, as letters to two churches. Interesting confirmation of this suggestion is to be found in the so-called Marcionite prefaces.[8] There is one preface *Ad Corinthios* and another, *Ad Thessalonicenses,* without the slightest hint that in each case not one, but two, epistles are being introduced. But when I and II Corinthians are taken together, and similarly I and II Thes-

[7] I thought this a "discovery" of my own until I came across a note in Harnack, *Marcion, Das Evangelium vom Fremden Gott* (Leipzig, 1921), p. 148 (1924 ed., 168-69).

[8] A convenient transcription of these prologues, found in many Latin MSS, appears in F. C. Burkitt, *The Gospel History and Its Transmission* (Edinburgh, 1911), pp. 353 ff. Many books on the New Testament canon also contain them. They were first identified as Marcionite by Dom D. de Bruyne, "Prologues bibliques d'Origine Marcionite," *Revue benedictine,* January, 1907. The prefaces to Corinthians and to Thessalonians, as rendered by Burkitt, are as follows:

"Corinthians are of Achaia. And these similarly heard the word of truth from the Apostle and were perverted variously by false apostles, some by the wordy eloquence of philosophy, others brought in by the sect of the Jewish law. These the Apostle recalls to the true evangelical wisdom, writing to them from Ephesus by Timothy."

"Thessalonians are Macedonians [in Christ Jesus], who having accepted the word of truth persevered in the faith even in persecution from their fellow-citizens. Moreover, also, they received not the things said by false apostles. These the Apostle praises, writing to them from Athens [by Timothy]."

salonians, the fact emerges that Marcion's list after Galatians names the letters roughly in the order of their length, beginning with the Corinthian correspondence and ending with Philemon. Would not the order of length have been a very natural one for the original publisher to adopt?

Several additional considerations buttress this supposition. One is the fact that the order of length would probably have been the most convenient order, when the scroll was used, since the longer and presumably more important letters would thus be the more easily accessible. Another is the fact that the tendency to arrange the letters of Paul in the order of their length seems to have been operative in the whole subsequent history of the canon. When Corinthians and Thessalonians came each to be thought of as two books (it is quite possible that they then became two books), Marcion's order would obviously no longer be the order of length. But in the various later lists and collections of the epistles one can see signs that the idea of arrangement in the order of length is at work like yeast until comparatively early our own list emerges, which, except that Ephesians and Galatians should be interchanged (an exception which, as we shall see, probably has significance), is determined by the length of the letters. But why this preoccupation with length in arranging the letters of Paul? One sees no sign of it in the Catholics or in the Gospels. Is it not simplest to account for it by the original order of the books in the Pauline collection?

It may be urged that the letters in Marcion's canon were plainly not altogether identical in content with the same letters as we know them and that it is quite possible that their comparative lengths were different. A moment's reflection, however, will reveal that the demonstration of any such variation would only strengthen the force of our suggestion as to the source of Marcion's order. For it is surely not accidental that the letters in Marcion's canon are arranged in the order of their length. He either invented that order or he inherited it. But if his changes within the letters were sufficiently extensive to alter their size relationships to one another as we know those same letters, it is clear that he could not himself have devised the order in which he places them. In other words, it is unthinkable that Marcion should accidentally have placed *his* letters in an order which only *our* letters can render logical. If he did so place them, he would necessarily have been following a more primitive arrangement.

It happens, however, that the order of length is not strictly adhered to in Marcion's list, and the apparent exceptions are very instructive. Disregarding Galatians, the position of which is satisfactorily explained, we notice two: Ephesians is clearly longer than Thessalonians (I and II), and Philippians seems to be longer than Colossians. When we examine the two latter, however, we find that it is only in the printed text that any difference in length appears. This is undoubtedly because Philippians contains a disproportionately large number of proper names which are regularly abbreviated in MSS but are, of course, printed in full. According to the traditional stichometry of the New Testament which Rendel Harris deduces from Euthalius and various codices containing verse measurements and which he verifies in remarkable fashion by his

own measurement of the printed text, the Pauline letters
fall into the following order:[9]

Corinthians (I and II)	1,460
Romans	920
Ephesians	312
Thessalonians (I and II)	299
Galatians	293
Colossians	208
Philippians	208
Philemon	38

Comparison of this list with Marcion's will show that
after Galatians the latter deviates at just one point: Ephesians follows Thessalonians when it "should" precede it.
Can we account for this variation? I venture to suggest
that we can. May it not be that Ephesians follows Thessalonians because it takes the place, left vacant, so to speak,
by Marcion's putting of Galatians in first position, the
position which Ephesians itself previously occupied? If the
original list was strictly in order of length, it began with
Corinthians, and Ephesians preceded, and Galatians followed, Thessalonians. But in that case, why should Marcion's lifting of Galatians out of its place disturb the
position of Ephesians? If, however, Ephesians headed the
first list and Marcion merely transposed it and Galatians,
the position of Ephesians in Marcion's canon is naturally
accounted for. The fact, to which attention has already
been called, that in our own list all that would be needed

[9] *Stichometry* (London, 1893), pp. 38 ff.

to bring the letters into strict order of length would be to transpose Galatians and Ephesians, is probably a sign of the importance of these two letters in the early history of the order of the epistles in the Pauline collection.

The view that when Marcion put Galatians at the beginning of his corpus, it took the place of another letter of about the same length which had previously been there is supported by the following consideration: The total number of *stichoi* in the letters of Paul is 3,738. Although it is conceivable that a single roll was made to hold the entire collection, it is almost certain that two rolls were used.[10] If this was the case, the one sure fact is that Corinthians and Romans were not on the same roll. Equally unlikely would be the putting of Corinthians on one roll and the rest of the letters on the other. As a matter of fact,

[10] For the ordinary size of rolls see F. G. Kenyon, *Books and Readers in Ancient Greece and Rome* (Oxford: Clarendon Press, 1932), pp. 61-62. My assumption that when the letters of Paul were first published the scroll form was used has been challenged by J. Finegan, "The Original Form of the Pauline Collection," *Harvard Theological Review* (1956), No. 2, 85-103. I do not see that Dr. Finegan has done more than demonstrate the *possibility* that the first Pauline letter collection was presented in codex form. It is true that scholarly researches have been pressing back to earlier and earlier times the first appearance of the codex, especially (it would seem) among Christians. But so far as I know, there is no clear evidence of its use in the first century. Even if such evidence should be found, however, the likelihood would still be that any particular book during that century was presented in the earlier traditional form. I ventured to make a brief reply to Dr. Finegan in the *Harvard Theological Review* of October, 1957, No. 4, 311-14. Dr. Finegan's article is valuable in citing much evidence from the early lists and "stichometries" in support of the view that the original order of the Pauline letters was, generally speaking, the order of length. A more adversely critical examination of this suggestion is made by C. H. Buck, Jr., "The Early Order of the Pauline Corpus," *Journal of Biblical Literature*, LXVIII (1949), 351 ff.

only one arrangement is possible at all—Corinthians and one of the smaller letters on one roll, and Romans and the other epistles on the second. But we have already seen reasons for believing that Ephesians headed the original corpus. Here, then, we have that view confirmed as well as a strong indication that it was followed by Corinthians.

It may be added that the publication of the corpus, divided after Ephesians and Corinthians, on two rolls would have this advantage: Romans, a long and important letter, would have headed the second volume of the collection. It would thus have an importance second only to that of Ephesians itself. The benediction at the end of II Corinthians, which has been regarded as a possible "finis" to the collection as a whole,[11] is now seen to be accounted for by the position of II Corinthians at the end of the first roll. It is attractive to surmise that Romans got the strange position it seems for a while to have occupied, at the end of the collection, at the time (no doubt earlier than has sometimes been thought) when the codex replaced the roll and the letters could all be published in a single book. Romans was too important a letter (and Rome was too important a church) to be buried in the heart of it. If it could not head the list, it would at least close it.

So far we have been assuming the accuracy of Tertullian's account of the order in which Marcion aranged the Pauline letters. But Epiphanius' account differs at one point, and it is now appropriate to examine that difference.

---

[11] Goodspeed, *New Solutions of New Testament Problems*, pp. 56-57.

According to Epiphanius, the Marcionite order was as follows;[12] Galatians, I Corinthians, II Corinthians, Romans, I Thessalonians, II Thessalonians, Ephesians, Colossians, Philemon, Philippians.

The question is, of course, about the position of Philemon. Did it follow Philippians or precede it? There are a number of reasons why we may lean toward the opinion that Epiphanius has preserved the more primitive arrangement.[13] The first is that he is more explicit about the order. He carefully designates the order of Marcion's epistles, differentiating it from the order which he favored. On two occasions he definitely numbers Philemon as IX and Philippians as X. Tertullian, on the other hand, says nothing about order, and our conclusion as to what he knew the Marcionite order to be is drawn only from the order in which he takes up the letters in his reply to Marcion. Moreover, he evidently did not regard the matter of order as significant, because although he vigorously assaults Marcion for mutilating the text and number of the epistles, he says nothing about order, although there is ample evidence that his own order differed substantially from Marcion's.[14] Besides, since he does not comment

[12] Epiphanius *Adv. Haer.*, Con. Marcionistas, ix ff. I disregard Epiphanius' confused and apparently mistaken references to an additional (eleventh) letter to the Laodiceans: ἐκεῖ δὲ καὶ τῆς πρὸς Λαοδικείας λεγομένης μέρη.

[13] According to H. A. Sanders' reconstruction, Philemon may have preceded Philippians in the Beatty Papyrus of the Pauline letters. *A Third Century Papyrus Codex of the Epistles of Paul* (Ann Arbor, Mich., 1935), p. 10.

[14] Zahn, *Geschichte des Neutestamentlichen Kanons* (Erlangen und Leipzig, 1890), II, 344 f.

84

upon Philemon, merely making a summary statement about it in the final paragraph of the whole work as being the only letter Marcion had not corrupted, it is by no means certain that he is not consciously taking it out of its order.

Two other considerations may incline us to favor Epiphanius' statement. One is the fact that Philippians would more probably have appealed to the original publishers as a strong and appropriate ending of the corpus than would Philemon. The other is the fact that since the idea of arrangement in order of length seems always to have been at work in collections of Paul's epistles, it is far easier to understand why, if Philemon was originally before Philippians, it should have dropped to its "proper" place at the end of the corpus, than why, if it originally occupied this "proper" place, it should have risen in the list. Philemon was probably "pulled" from its original position between Colossians and Philippians, when the Pastorals become a part of the Pauline collection and it was able to take a place as a personal letter among other personal letters, as well as serve, perhaps, to integrate the Pastorals more closely into the traditional Pauline collection.

But, if Epiphanius' order is the more original in this respect, how can we account for it? Clearly in only one possible way. Originally, and also in Marcion's period, Colossians and Philemon sustained with each other a relation of more than usual closeness. They were in some unique way companion letters and would not be separated. In other words, the two letters which we have found to be so closely related to each other in original occasion and purpose, are now seen to have been preserved together as well. It will be recalled that in our examination of Tertullian's evidence we were at first disturbed by what appeared to be the irregular placing of Colossians before Philippians. We tried to explain it by showing that while apparently longer, Philippians was of exactly equal length according to the traditional stichometry. Nevertheless, the fact that in most other lists Philippians precedes Colossians at least suggests that among the ancients, as with us, Philippians was thought of as being the longer letter. We see now that this counting of syllables to show that Colossians is barely as long as Philippians was unnecessary. Its priority is otherwise much more convincingly accounted for. It preceded Philippians because it was accompanied by Philemon. For Colossians-Philemon is thirty-eight *stichoi* longer than Philippians and is forty-seven *stichoi* shorter than Galatians, which doubtless next preceded it in the list. We believe, then, that we are justified in feeling a considerable measure of assurance that when the letters of Paul were published late in the first century, they were arranged as follows: Ephesians (general letter), Corinthians, Romans, Thessalonians, Galatians, Colossians, Philemon, Philippians.

III

May I conclude this discussion of order in the primitive corpus by calling attention to a fact which may be merely curious, but may possibly be significant. We have thus far been occupied in reconstructing the original corpus by observing the arrangement of the Marcionite corpus. But we possess a second list, at least a half century later than Marcion's, but still very early—the so-called Muratorian canon.[15] In this list the letters of Paul are placed in the following order: Corinthians, Ephesians, Philippians, Colossians, Galatians, Thessalonians, and Romans. We are also told that Paul wrote to Philemon, to Titus, and twice to Timothy, and that there were two letters to the Corinthians and two to the Thessalonians. What are we to make of this second most ancient arrangement? I think it is fair to say that it does not at any point prove the falseness of the reconstruction of the primitive corpus I have been proposing and that in some ways it clearly confirms it. The point of particular importance here is that Galatians is in the center of the list and that Ephesians, which almost certainly headed the first collection,[16] is second only to Corinthians, which in the hypothesis originally preceded it. That Ephesians, the shorter letter, should have dropped beneath Corinthians is understandable, especially when it

[15] For the text of this second-century document see B. F. Westcott, *A General Survey of the History of the Canon of the New Testament* (London: Macmillan and Company, 1896) ; H. Lietzmann, *Das Muratorische Fragment* (Bonn: Marcus and Weber, 1908) ; or virtually any of the current compendia of selected early Christian documents, such as those of H. M. Gwatkin, J. Stevenson, and others.

[16] Perhaps it should be pointed out that even if Ephesians is regarded as a genuine letter of Paul, this position for it in the original collection is strongly indicated. Where in a collection of church letters, each with some such title as "To the Thessalonians" or "To the Philippians," would the editor have placed a letter without particular church address—where except at the beginning? And the contents of the letter suit it for that position quite regardless of who wrote it. In other words Professor Goodspeed's proposal as to the original position of Ephesians in the collection can be accepted—and it seems to me, needs to be—even by those who find all the rest of his hypothesis unacceptable.

87

came to be thought of as "Ephesians" rather than as a general letter; and that Philemon should have been pulled away from its close association with Colossians in order to take its place as a personal note with the newly incorporated notes to Timothy and Titus—this also was to be expected. But what can one make of the order of the other letters: Philippians, Colossians, Galatians, Thessalonians, Romans? Perhaps this is the result of an effort to place the letters in their chronological order; but one makes the suggestion only to reject it, for is it likely that Philippians in that case would have been assigned so high a place in the list? I have no solution to propose with assurance, but I cannot refrain from calling attention to a very curious fact: if, as we have seen reason to believe, the original collection was published on two rolls—Ephesians and Corinthians on one of them and Romans, Thessalonians, Galatians, Colossians-Philemon, and Philippians on the other—it is interesting to observe that the order of the Muratorian list is the exact opposite of this order. Is it possible that some early scribe copied the letters in reverse order, or at any rate their names? [17] This supposition may appear altogether too fanciful, but that our earliest list of the letters of Paul—that of Marcion—has indicated an order in the original collection which our next earliest list exactly reverses is, to say the least, interesting. And this fact does not become less striking when it

[17] F. G. Kenyon ("Papyrus Rolls and the ending of Mark," *Journal of Theological Studies* XL [1939], 56 ff.) has pointed out that rolls, when not in use, would probably stand as the latest readers left them—that is, with the ending, rather than the beginning, exposed. This fact may be relevant in the present connection.

is remarked that the Muratorian order of the "personal" epistles in the Pauline corpus seems also to be in reverse—Philemon, Titus, Timothy. That Philemon is placed before the Pastorals is not unnatural—although I do not believe there is another ancient list in which this is true—but that Titus precedes Timothy is certainly surprising. A diagram may perhaps help here:

MARCION	ORIGINAL	MURATORIAN
Galatians	Ephesians	Corinthians
Corinthians	Corinthians	Ephesians
Romans	Romans	Philippians
Thessalonians	Thessalonians	Colossians
Ephesians	Galatians	Galatians
Colossians	Colossians	Thessalonians
Philemon	Philemon	Romans
Philippians	Philippians	
		Philemon
		Titus
		Timothy

Is it possible to construct hypothetically another original order from which our two earliest known orders can as plausibly be derived?

However hypothetical some of this discussion of order in the original Pauline letter collection has necessarily been, I hope that in the course of it I have succeeded at least in demonstrating the strong probability that from the beginning Philemon was a part of the Pauline tradition and that it was closely associated in that tradition with

Colossians. It may be added that in whatever way one may reconstruct the earlier history of the collection of the letters of Paul, the fact that in the time of Marcion Philemon was a member of the corpus is itself almost sufficient proof that it had always belonged to it. For Philemon is not the kind of letter which would have been subsequently added. But this brings us to the last and culminating question of this study: What is the meaning of the presence of Philemon in the published church letters of Paul?

CHAPTER V

———•———

The Historical Importance of Philemon

I

SO FAR WE HAVE DEALT WITH THE MERELY MECHANICAL position of Philemon in the primitive collection of the Pauline letters. But what about the more important matter of its organic connection—of its rôle and function in the corpus? What is its significance there? What is the meaning of the presence in a collection of church letters of a certain characteristic type of this note so unlike the others in size, address, and content? Jerome tells us that many of his contemporaries objected to Philemon's inclusion in the New Testament canon, not because it was unauthentic, but because it was, as compared with the other epistles, trivial.[1] Tertullian implies not a little disparagement of Philemon when he writes about it, "I wonder, however, when he [Marcion] admitted this letter which was written but to a man, that he rejected the two epistles to Timothy and the one to Titus, which all treat of ecclesiastical discipline." [2] For Tertullian, Philemon is a rather slight work,

[1] Preface to Philemon.
[2] *Adv. Marcion.* v. 21.

even as compared with the Pastorals. But when the collection was made, it could have had the benefit of no such comparison. The contrast between it and the other letters would have appeared stark and unqualified. Why, then, was it included?

It is well to realize at the outset of this part of our discussion the importance of that question. The more anomalous the presence of Philemon in the collection appears, the more significant must it be. The more grounds can be cited for its exclusion, the more important must have been the ground upon which it was actually included. The very fact that Philemon seems so out of place is evidence that the original editors had very good reason for including it. We can be sure that if we knew that reason we should know something very important indeed about the publication of the Pauline letters. It is worth while, then, to inquire: Why was Philemon included in the corpus of church letters, ascribed to Paul, which was published (probably at Ephesus) near the end of the first century?

First of all, one may point out that its place in Marcion's list would seem to indicate that Philemon in the primitive collection did not have quite the status of the other letters but occupied a position somewhat subordinate to that of Colossians. Goodspeed writes, "Philemon may have stood as a separate letter, but was more probably attached to Colossians, since the seven-fold character of the list in its early form seems to have been an outstanding feature of it." [3] The arrangement of the letters in Marcion's canon

---

[3] *Formation of the New Testament,* p. 30.

fully confirms this suggestion. It was almost without question a corpus of seven units, Colossians and Philemon being taken together. This close affiliation of the two letters was all but inevitable—not only were they written and delivered at the same time, and, we believe, to the same community, but Philemon is actually alluded to in the Colossian epistle. The subordination of Philemon, as the briefer, more personal note, to the longer, more typical church letter was equally natural. But although it is undoubtedly easier to understand the inclusion of Philemon if it was thus subordinated than as an altogether independent epistle, this fact hardly *accounts* for its inclusion. We are enabled better to see *how* it could have been done, but not *why* it should have been done, for Philemon clearly did not lose its identity as a separate letter.

Because of this difficulty Professor Goodspeed has more recently made the suggestion that the motive for including Philemon may well have been, at least in part, the desire to have the corpus contain letters to seven churches and that Philemon was originally entitled *To the Laodiceans*. The fact that Revelation contains, after a general address, letters to seven churches and that the church at Laodicea was one of these gives weight to the suggestion.[4] Attractive as it unquestionably is, however, its acceptance involves certain difficulties of importance. One is the fact that if it bore the title "Laodiceans," it is not easy to understand why it should have been coupled with Colossians in quite so close a way as the phenomena of Marcion's list would

[4] Goodspeed, *New Solutions of New Testament Problems*, pp. 51 ff.

indicate. Another is the fact that although it is, no doubt, the letter referred to as "from Laodicea," it almost certainly was not addressed (except perhaps for Philemon himself) to Laodiceans,[5] and could scarcely have been so regarded a few decades later. Again, although Philemon is directed to "the church that meets in your house," in its address and whole character it is so different from the other church letters that one finds it difficult to think of it as analogous to them, and one suspects that the ancients would have felt similarly. Finally, and most decisively, there is the silent testimony of Marcion.

Marcion, as we have seen, reflects the primitive corpus with great completeness and accuracy, but he knows nothing of Philemon's having been called "Laodiceans." We are sure of that because he gives that title to another letter altogether—the introductory general letter, which he brings down into the body of the collection of church letters and for which, therefore, he is forced to find a church name. He fastened upon this name partly because of Col. 4:16 and partly, no doubt, under the influence of a continuing tradition in the church (for which there is other evidence) [6] that a letter to the Laodiceans had been written. But if there was a letter to the Laodiceans in the primitive corpus, why may it not have been the letter which Paul explicitly directs shall be sent there—our Colossians? It is more than possible that the first title of Colossians-Philemon was *To the Colossians and the Laodiceans*. I have already referred to the so-called "Marcionite

[5] See above, pp. 48-55.
[6] Goodspeed, *op. cit.*, pp. 62-63.

Latin prologues." It is a matter of special notice among the scholars who have investigated these undoubtedly early prefaces and of some speculation, that in one of them (and in one only) two churches are named, the Colossians and the Laodiceans.[7] This may well be a relic of the ancient title of Colossians and Philemon. There would thus have been a collection of seven letters to seven churches. I do not wish to insist upon the point, but I can hardly refrain from adding that if the name "Laodiceans" had this rather tenuous, second-hand hold upon one of the letters, it is not difficult to understand why it soon dropped out and also why later the notion seems to have been extant that a *Laodiceans* of about the length of our Philemon had belonged to the corpus.[8] A twofold book with a twofold title might lead to any number of later confusions. But this is largely speculative. There seem to be solid grounds, however, for questioning the hypothesis that at the beginning Philemon was published as the Epistle to the Laodiceans.

As a matter of fact, we can conceive of no adequate ground for the inclusion of Philemon except a personal one. Some personal consideration must be held to account for the compiler's incorporating among the Pauline letters this personal note. I shall not now attempt to be more specific, but it is worth remembering that Philemon was

[7] See, for example, the article of De Bruyne already referred to and Peter Corssen, "Zur Überlieferungsgeschichte des Römerbriefes," *Zeitschrift für die Neuestestamentliche Wissenschaft,* X, 42. This particular preface begins, "Colosenses et hi, sicut Laodicenses, sunt Asiani."

[8] Goodspeed (*op. cit.,* pp. 52-53) points out that the spurious "Laodiceans" found in many Latin MSS of the New Testament is of the same length as Philemon.

certainly a very important document for at least one person, and that this person probably became an active worker in the Pauline churches.

One additional remark in this connection is in order. That the compiler of the corpus was in some way responsible for Ephesians, Goodspeed has in my judgment amply proved. The case rests largely upon the demonstrable fact that Ephesians shows the influence of all of the other letters which belonged to the collection. But although the author of this encyclical, designed to introduce the corpus, used all of the extant epistles, he made quite the largest use of Colossians.[9] This is so strikingly true that Ephesians has sometimes been regarded as a kind of "second edition" of Colossians, absorbing as it does so large a proportion of the other letter. But why this dominating influence of Colossians upon the writer of Ephesians? I can think of no answer to that question except that he knew or liked Colossians best, in either case, a personal consideration. But here is a remarkable fact—the two letters in the collection, in which, for quite independent reasons we have decided, the compiler had some particular personal interest, are the same two letters which we have already seen to be closely related to each other in almost every other possible way—Colossians and Philemon. Can this be accidental? Does not the indisputable personal interest of the author of Ephesians in Colossians confirm the view that

[9] See Clayton R. Bowen, " 'Ephesians' among the Letters of Paul," *ATR* (October, 1933) , p. 287; Goodspeed, *The Meaning of Ephesians,* Part II; and C. L. Mitton, *Epistle to the Ephesians,* pp. 55 ff. James Moffatt (*Introduction to the Literature of the New Testament,* p. 393) calls Ephesians "a catholicised version of Colossians."

it was a personal interest of the compiler of the corpus in Philemon which largely accounts for its membership in the primitive collection?

As to the place of the collection, by far the most likely is Ephesus, although Corinth has also been proposed.[10] The arguments for Ephesus have been ably marshalled by Goodspeed in the several books already cited and in a chapter on the early literary importance of Ephesus in his *New Chapters in New Testament Study*.[11] Attention may also be called to the fact that Ephesus seems to have been Paul's principal headquarters and might have been expected to serve as the base for the collection of his literary remains. The fact that the Marcionite prologues describe three (or four) of the letters as having been written from Ephesus may be cited as evidence of an early tradition associating Paul's letters as a whole with that city. Such a tradition would explain the absence of an "Ephesians" from the earliest corpus, as well as Ignatius' phrase, "in

[10] Zahn, *op. cit.*, I, 837; Harnack, *op. cit.*, pp. 8 ff. I have made some attempt at refuting such case as there is for Corinth in *Marcion and the New Testament*, pp. 174 ff. P. N. Harrison (*Polycarp's Two Epistles to the Philippians*, pp. 238 ff.) tries to take account of the claims of both cities: the job of collecting was begun from Corinth and finished in Ephesus. See also K. Lake's argument that there were several independent primitive collections of Paul's letters (*The Earlier Epistles of St. Paul* [London: Rivingtons, 1911], pp. 356 ff.).

[11] New York: The Macmillan Company, 1937. One does not need to find each of Goodspeed's arguments convincing in order to recognize that he makes altogether a strong case. Even scholars need sometimes to be reminded that in matters of this kind the proverb to the effect that a chain is no stronger than its weakest link does not apply. A weak argument may not help—or help much—but it should not be regarded as hurting one's case. And even the weaker arguments may have an important cumulative effect.

every letter he remembers you." [12] Also the strange and pre-eminent importance of Ephesians, Colossians, and Philemon for the collector suggests Ephesus, or at any rate an Asian city. The fact that the general covering letter came to be called "Ephesians" points in the same direction. Every consideration, in fact, a priori and historical favors Ephesus.

We have, thus, a Paulinist, probably of Ephesus, with a close acquaintance with Colossians and a personal connection of some kind with Philemon, who was influential in the publication of the Pauline letter collection in the last decade of the first century. I believe that yet another very important step in the direction of the identification of this individual can be taken with a considerable measure of confidence. I am convinced that a connection can be established between Philemon and one of the letters of Ignatius, a connection which not only confirms the view proposed here of the original purpose of Philemon but also throws a flood of light upon the earliest stage in the development of the New Testament canon.

II

One of the victims of the local persecutions of Christians which took place in various parts of the Roman Empire during the principate of Trajan was Ignatius, the bishop of Antioch in Syria. He was sent under arrest to Rome, where in all probability he suffered martyrdom. His itinerary lay through Asia Minor, and there seem to have been halts of some length in the cities of Smyrna and

[12] See Goodspeed, *New Solutions of New Testament Problems,* p. 8.

Troas. In any case, from these cities he wrote several letters, for the most part to churches, and from them we derive virtually all the knowledge we have of this early martyr.

It is the letter to the church at Ephesus which particularly interests us. Strikingly enough, the bishop of this church is named Onesimus, and Ignatius' epistle contains many laudatory references to him. Onesimus had evidently gone to Smyrna to visit Ignatius and had taken with him other representatives of the Ephesian church—Burrhus, Crocus, Euplus, and Fronto are named. Ignatius wants Burrhus, and perhaps Crocus, to stay with him, and all but begins his letter with this request. His whole manner of making it is interesting: περὶ δὲ τοῦ συνδούλου Βούρρου, τοῦ κατὰ θεὸν διακόνου ὑμῶν ἐν πᾶσιν εὐλογημένου, εὔχομαι παραμεῖναι αὐτὸν εἰς τιμὴν ὑμῶν καὶ τοῦ ἐπισκόπου (Eph. 2:1: "As for my fellow servant Burrhus, your deacon by God's will and blessed in all things, I ask that he remain with me for your honor and that of the bishop"). The similarity of this sentence to one of the sentences in Philemon is obvious (Philem. 13). It is true that Paul writes ἐβουλόμην and Ignatius uses the word εὔχομαι; that Paul says, ὃν . . . κατέχειν, while Ignatius chooses to say, παραμεῖναι αὐτόν; that Paul writes ὑπέρ σου and Ignatius, εἰς τιμὴν ὑμῶν. But such differences are merely verbal; besides, they are more than offset, perhaps, by the occurrence in the passage of the term διακόνου (cf. διακονῇ in Philem. 13) and of συνδούλου, a word surely suggestive of Philemon and found in Paul only in Colossians, where it appears twice. Having in this way been led to think of Philemon, we are not surprised to find Ignatius in the very next sentence asserting that Crocus has relieved him, using the word ἀνέπαυσεν (cf. Philem. 7 and 20). He goes on immediately to express the hope that he may "make something" out of the Ephesians, employing the optative ὀναίμην (cf. Philem. 20), the occurrence of which here, whether a play on the name of the bishop is being made or not, is very striking in view of the other indications of the influence of Philemon upon Ignatius' style in the four sentences of this second chapter.

But it is the even shorter third chapter that this influence is perhaps most decisively indicated: Οὐ διατάσσομαι ὑμῖν ὡς ὤν τις. Εἰ γὰρ καὶ δέδεμαι ἐν τῷ ὀνόματι, οὔπω ἀπήρτισμαι . . . ἀλλ' ἐπεὶ ἡ ἀγάπη οὐκ ἐᾷ με σιωπᾶν . . . διὰ τοῦτο . . . προέλαβον παρακαλεῖν ὑμᾶς ("I do not command you as though I were Somebody. For even if I am a prisoner for the Name, I have not yet been made perfect . . . but since love does not permit me to be silent . . . therefore . . . I am taking it on myself to appeal to you").

The resemblance of this passage to Philem. 8 and 9 is too clear to need pointing out. Paul had written that although he felt he had ample right to make demands— was he not Paul (τοιοῦτος ὡς Παῦλος) ambassador [13] of Christ and now even a prisoner for him?—yet because of love he preferred to appeal. Ignatius denies that he has the right to command, even though he is a prisoner "for

---

[13] That this is the meaning of πρεσβύτης here is now widely acknowledged. See Lightfoot, *op. cit.*, p. 336.

the name," but love compels him to appeal to his readers. The correspondence of ἐπιτάσσειν and διατάσσομαι, τοιοῦτος ὢν ὡς and ὡς ὢν τις, δέσμιος and δέδεμαι, διὰ τὴν ἀγάπην and ἀγάπη . . . διὰ τοῦτο and finally παρακαλῶ and παρακαλεῖν cannot in our opinion be fortuitous.[14]

All of these reminiscences of Philemon are found in chapters 2 and 3, but other chapters of Ignatius' letter to the Ephesians contain indications almost as clear. In the first chapter one finds πίστιν καὶ ἀγάπην ἐν Χριστῷ 'Ιησοῦ ("faith and love in Christ Jesus"; cf. Philem. 5) and ἐλπίζοντα τῇ προσευχῇ ὑμῶν ("hoping by your prayer"; cf. Philem. 22), and in the latter instance the proximity in both Philemon and Ignatius of the word χαρίζειν may not be without significance. In chapter 4 it is by no means impossible that ἀκούσῃ καὶ ἐπιγινώσκῃ δι' ὧν εὖ πράσσετε ("that he may hear and recognize through the good things you do") has some connection with Philem. 5-6: ἀκούων . . . ἐν ἐπιγνώσει παντὸς ἀγαθοῦ. Chapter 5 begins in a manner strikingly suggestive of Philem. 15-16: Εἰ γὰρ ἐγὼ ἐν μικρῷ χρόνῳ τοιαύτην συνήθειαν ἔσχον πρὸς τὸν ἐπίσκοπον ὑμῶν, οὐκ ἀνθρωπίνην οὖσαν, ἀλλὰ πνευματικήν, πόσῳ μᾶλλον ὑμᾶς μακαρίζω. . . . (For if in a little while I have had this kind of communion—not human, but spiritual—with your bishop, how much more do I congratulate you.") And in chapter 6, ὃν πέμπει . . . δεῖ ἡμᾶς αὐτὸν δέχεσθαι, ὡς αὐτὸν τὸν πέμψαντα ("whom he sends . . . him ought we to receive as we would the one who sent him") cannot

[14] H. J. Holtzmann acknowledges that this passage "an Philemon 8-9 anklingt," *op. cit.*, p. 431. So also does C. R. Gregory, *The Canon and Text of the New Testament* (New York, 1907), p. 210.

fail to remind one of Philem. 17. In a word, every one of the first six chapters of Ignatius' Epistle to the Ephesians contains some expression definitely reminiscent of Philemon. I am far from insisting that each of these citations represents a clear case of literary influence; perhaps no one of them standing alone would be altogether convincing. I do claim, however, that all of them taken together, particularly in view of their concentration in the first six short paragraphs of a single letter, can be accounted for only upon the assumption of some literary connection.[15]

The striking character of this use of Philemon by Ignatius it is impossible to exaggerate. It is altogether anomalous. Nowhere (outside the Pauline corpus itself)[16] in the whole range of extant early Christian literature is it to be matched in any measure whatever. Occasionally, beginning with Tertullian,[17] references are made to the epistle by name and eventually commentaries begin to be written on it, but nowhere is such acquaintance with its language and style reflected in another composition. One is not surprised at this fact. Philemon is too local and particular and personal to enjoy the use which the more "religious" and more widely significant church letters of Paul soon enjoyed. The phenomena in Ignatius' Ephe-

[15] Many contemporary scholars agree with this judgment. I cited in the Preface E. J. Goodspeed, A. E. Barnett, and P. N. Harrison in this connection.

[16] The language of Philemon is reflected in Colossians and in Ephesians, and quite possibly in the Pastorals. But the Pastorals, like Ephesians, are consciously based on the available Pauline letters as such, so that their use of Philemon is naturally accounted for. The original connection of Colossians and Philemon has been discussed.

[17] See above, pp. 91 ff.

sians which we have cited are, then, altogether amazing. We should not expect Philemon to be quoted, and we do not find it quoted with this single impressive exception. Why should Ignatius alone have made use of Philemon, and he such large use of it? It is hard to escape the conclusion that the same fact which accounts for the neglect of the epistle by others explains its use by him—the personal nature of the contents of the letter.

When one reaches this point in the consideration of the significance of this evidence, one finds it hard to dismiss as mere coincidence the fact that the name of the bishop of the church at Ephesus, to which Ignatius is writing, was Onesimus. We are even less likely to do so when we observe that in the first six chapters of Ignatius' letter are fourteen references to Onesimus either by name or office, and that in the other fifteen chapters no reference to him is made at all, and only one to the bishop's office. As a matter of fact, Onesimus is the real subject of these six chapters, and it is these chapters only which show traces of Philemon's influence. This can hardly be accidental; the implication is clear that for Ignatius there was some connection between Philemon and the bishop Onesimus. What could this connection have been? One hesitates to adopt the obvious answer—it would seem too simple to be true—that the Onesimus of Ignatius and of Paul was the same individual. And yet, why not? Paul's Onesimus would not necessarily have been too old in 107, or even in 117, to be bishop of Ephesus. Paul was quite probably in Ephesus when he asked for Onesimus' release. Whether he was there or not at the time, Ephesus was a very natural place for this Asian Christian to work—it had long been Paul's primary headquarters. That the slave Onesimus was a person of promise is indicated by Paul's great concern to have him with him. It would have been natural for places of leadership in the Pauline churches to be held by the actual companions of Paul himself so long as there were any of them living. That some were living when Ignatius wrote is perhaps indicated by the twelfth chapter of his letter where the Ephesians are described as "fellow-priests" or "fellow-initiates" of Paul. Why may not the bishop of Ephesus have been primarily in Ignatius' mind when he wrote that? [18]

But in almost conclusive support of this suggestion I call attention to a highly interesting sentence in the first chapter of Ignatius' letter. After greeting the church, he writes as follows:

'Αποδεξάμενος ἐν θεῷ τὸ πολυαγάπητόν σου ὄνομα, ὃ κέκτησθε φύσει δικαίᾳ κατὰ πίστιν καὶ ἀγάπην ἐν Χριστῷ 'Ιησοῦ, τῷ σωτῆρι ἡμῶν· μιμηταὶ ὄντες θεοῦ, ἀναζωπυρήσαντες ἐν αἵματι θεοῦ τὸ συγγενικὸν ἔργον τελείως ἀπηρτίσατε· ἀκούσαντες γὰρ δεδεμένον ἀπὸ Συρίας ὑπὲρ τοῦ κοινοῦ ὀνόματος καὶ ἐλπίδος, . . . ἰδεῖν ἐσπουδάσατε· ἐπεὶ οὖν τὴν πολυπληθίαν ὑμῶν ἐν ὀνόματι θεοῦ ἀπείληφα ἐν 'Ονησίμῳ. . . . ("I have welcomed in God your much loved name, which you have obtained by your righteous nature according to faith and love in Christ Jesus our Savior. Being imitators of God, you have kindled in the blood of God your congenital task and have completed it perfectly. For hearing that I had been sent a

---

[18] I have not referred to the tradition that identifies Paul's Onesimus with Ignatius,' since its origins are not known.

prisoner from Syria for our common name and hope . . . you hastened to visit me. Since, then, I have received your whole number in the person of Onesimus. . . .")

This passage has always given difficulty to the interpreter. Why is the singular pronoun σου employed? Why is the church at Ephesus said to have obtained its dear name because of its righteous nature? Does "name" here mean "reputation"? Would it then be natural to characterize it as "dear" or "much-loved"? Does it mean "character"? In that case, is it natural to continue with the remark that the Ephesians have secured it by their righteous nature? Besides the word ὄνομα in Ignatius seems everywhere else to mean "name" in the more ordinary sense.[19] And why such a quasi-technical word as φύσις? Similar questions make the phrase τὸ συγγενικὸν ἔργον difficult. Lake,[20] following Zahn, translates this adjective "brotherly"; Lightfoot prefers "natural" or "congenial," although he acknowledges that the word really means "congenital." [21] But what does Ignatius means by the Ephesians' *"congenital work"*? And what is this "work" (ἔργον) ? Is it merely showing kindness to people in need? If so, how can it be said that they have "completed" it? All of these questions and more are raised by Ignatius' language when one undertakes to interpret it as applying to the church at Ephesus.

But let us suppose that Ignatius is really thinking of the bishop, and of the church only as it was represented in

[19] Notice especially Mag. 1:2; Rom. 10:1; Smyr. 13:2; Poly. 8:3. These all refer to personal names, usually "dear to me."

[20] K. Lake, *The Apostolic Fathers* (London, 1930) , *ad loc.*

[21] J. B. Lightfoot, *The Apostolic Fathers* (London, 1885) , *ad loc.*

him. This supposition is in no way extravagant. Ignatius
loves to exalt the bishop and tends to identify the bishop
and the church. Besides, in this passage he explicitly says
that it was *in the person of Onesimus* that he thinks of
himself as having received the whole congregation. Thus,
it is clear that in saying "You hastened to see me," he is
really alluding to Onesimus' visit. I submit that in the
whole of the first two sentences he was addressing himself
symbolically to the church at Ephesus, but concretely to
its bishop. Does he not say as much?

But if this is true, the "difficult" passage not only ceases
to be difficult, it becomes illuminating indeed. *"Thy* very
dear name" is "Onesimus," with which Ignatius had already been "favorably acquainted." Onesimus had "obtained it by his righteous nature," and one remembers
Paul's words: τοῦ ἐμοῦ τέκνου, ὃν ἐγέννησα ἐν τοῖς δεσμοῖς
᾽Ονήσιμον, τὸν πότε . . . ἄχρηστον νυνὶ δὲ . . . εὔχρηστον
(Philem. 10-11). The mystical term ἀναζωπυρήσαντες is
another reference to the spiritual rebirth of a certain slave
of many years ago. There can be little doubt that the
phrase μιμηταὶ ὄντες θεοῦ ("being imitators of God") had
also a sacramental sense.[22] And what about the "congenital
work"? How appropriate this phrase, if it applied to one

---

[22] In striking confirmation of this I call attention to Eph. 5:1: γίνεσθε
οὖν μιμηταὶ τοῦ θεοῦ, ὡς τέκνα ἀγαπητά, and more particularly to I Cor.
4:14 f.: οὐκ ἐντρέπων ὑμᾶς γράφω ταῦτα, ἀλλ᾽ ὡς τέκνα μου ἀγαπητὰ
νουθετῶν. ᾽Εὰν γὰρ μυρίους παιδαγωγοὺς ἔχητε ἐν Χριστῷ, ἀλλ᾽ οὐ πόλλους
πατέρας, ἐν γὰρ Χριστῷ ᾽Ιησοῦ διὰ τοῦ εὐαγγελίου ἐγὼ ὑμᾶς ἐγέννησα.
παρακαλῶ οὖν ὑμᾶς, μιμηταί μου γίνεσθε. Διὰ τοῦτο ἔπεμψα ὑμῖν Τιμόθεον,
ὅς ἐστίν μου τέκνον ἀγαπητὸν καὶ πιστὸν ἐν κυρίῳ. It is interesting to note
that it is only in this passage and in Philemon that Paul refers to an
individual as his "child."

who had been "born" to be "useful"—and not only so in a general sense, but useful particularly to a certain prisoner for the good news, with whom Ignatius more than once compares himself! "I have known and loved your very dear name," says Ignatius, "which you received because of your righteous nature; and, an imitator of God, renewing your nature through his blood, you have now brought the work you were born to do to an appropriate consummation, for when you heard that *I* was a prisoner . . . you hastened to visit me." Could we want a clearer indication of the identity of Paul's and Ignatius' Onesimus? The letter to Philemon is the key to the understanding of the opening paragraphs of Ignatius' letter to the Ephesians.

But if Onesimus, the slave whom Paul asked from his master for a career of religious service, was the bishop of Ephesus about A.D. 110, it is altogether likely that he held the same office a score of years earlier. If so, he was at Ephesus when a corpus of Paul's letters was published; indeed, that publication would probably have been done under his oversight. And what better explanation would we need of both the presence of Philemon in the collection and the predominant influence of Colossians upon the maker of Ephesians?

Although final proof of this hypothesis must wait for further evidence, I submit that the facts in our possession render it exceedingly plausible. It confirms other indications as to the place and period of the primitive Pauline letter-collection and provides a very convincing motive for its creation. For Onesimus would have been a Paulinist, and the collection would have been the devoted "service"

107

of a grateful disciple. He would thus have never ceased to be "useful" to his master, even though his work soon dropped from sight and was forgotten.

III

With this publication of the Pauline letters the history of the New Testament, as a fixed collection of books, properly begins. It was Marcion's appropriation of this corpus a half-century later and his setting it up as the major part of a new "Bible," which should take the place for his followers of the Jewish Scriptures, generally acknowledged by the churches, that gave the decisive impulse toward the formation of the New Testament, as a second formal and authorized canon. That the name of Paul stands affixed to fully one-third of the contents of that canon is due also to that fact. If the proposal defended in these pages should prove to be valid, it is, perhaps, not too much to say that the brief note to Philemon, often despised and ignored in the history of New Testament study, may well be from the standpoint of the story of the canon the most significant single book in the New Testament—the living link between the Pauline career and the Pauline tradition, between the letters of Paul and the New Testament of the church.

Index of Authors Cited